Stories of Men, Meaning and Prayer

STORIES OF
MEN,
MEANING
AND
PRAYER

THE RECONCILIATION OF HEART AND SOUL
IN MODERN MANHOOD

JEFFREY DUVALL
WITH JAMES CHURCHES

Prayer is anything that connects us to meaning, that helps us believe in ourselves and our purposes, that sustains a faith in life and nature, that connects us to our blood lineage, our children, elders, partners and communities; anything that serves in this way is prayer, is sacred, beloved and full of grace.

—Fools Crow, Lakota medicine man

FOUR DIRECTIONS PRESS

FIRST EDITION, NOVEMBER 2001

Published by Four Directions Press, P.O. Box 813, Nederland, CO 80466

Printed by Print Communications Group, Inc., 175 Rte. 46 W., Fairfield, NJ 07004

Library of Congress Cataloging-in-Publication Data

Duvall, Jeffrey, 1953-

Stories of men meaning and prayer: the reconciliation of heart and soul in modern manhood / Jeffrey Duvall with James Churches. - 1st. ed.

ISBN 0-9711423-0-0

Library of Congress Control Number: 2001118869

1. Developmental psychology 2. Rites, rituals and ceremonies
3. Spiritual life (nature) 4. Initiation 5. Men's Studies

Set in Adobe Garamond
Book Design: Standing Stone Design
Cover Design: Ted and Peggy Warren
Cover photo: Rajan Kose/Standing Stone Productions, ©1989, 2000
Art and photography:
    Michael Kimball: block print on page 62
    Rajan Kose/Standing Stone Productions: photos on pages 102,140, ©2000
    Ted Warren: drawing on page 38
    Jack West: drawing on page 124
    Jeffrey Duvall: photos on pages 14, 40, 80, 162

To order books (quantity discounts available), inquire into sponsoring a program in your area or for information about Jeffrey Duvall's schedule of retreats and trainings you can contact him by email at: jpd@peakpeak.com or write to him at: PO Box 813, Nederland, CO 80466.

Dedicated to
Mary and Luke
in heart and gratitude
always

Acknowledgments

In gratitude for my ancestors. For grandmothers Marie and Edith, for grandfathers Curtis and Louie. For my parents Virginia and Marvin Duvall for their gift of life and loving support. For the rest of my family: Michael, Terri, and Chris for hanging in with me. For the strong blood and heart we share.

For my prayerful godparents Laura and Robert Dunbar. To the river Raisin and Lake Superior for their fierce and gentle beauty in each season.

To art and heart advisors Peggy and Ted Warren, Snowflake, Alice Treadway, Hilda Rasmussen, Bishop Robert, Doctor Herman, Tom Daly, David Phillips, Robert Bly, Doris and Airic Leonardson, Robert Cote, Bruce Rose, John Guarnaschelli, Bob Bernard, Mel Grusing—elders who touch deeply.

For Mark Hochwender, the Root Kiva, Pipe Stone Lodge and Spruce Tree Lodge and Sapphire Canyon. Meredith Little, Steven Foster, Judith Snow, Sarah McKoy and Mariom Kessler.

To Keith Fairmont, Michael Kimball, Larry Lammers, Larry Tassiday, Jim Carbone, Joe Laur, Dick Busanyi, Gurudarshon Khalsa, Colby Lewis, Colleen and James Purcaro for their incredible love and support, vision and faith. To the Berkshire Men's Council, the Minnesota friends, Mountain Men Circle, Brad Gallup, Lucas Hendrickson, Frank Evans, Blue Joy a'Singin', Terry Fitzgerald, Ron Kerns, Ken Cohen, Peter Korba, Ray Gobeille, John Davis, Nancy Jane, Jack West, Michael Hodgkins, Cass Adams, John Calvi, James Sargent, David Ruskay, Terry Cohen and Seth Henry. And to the many I have missed here of no less importance—you have all kept me alive.

For all the men who came to the many gatherings and shared their stories and dared to risk the inquiry—the pains and graces of evolving manhood in the grand dance of life, death and the evolution of heart and soul—your stories are the spirit of this book, thank you.

For all young people—you are beautiful, and for those I have shared heart, mystery and story with. You have broken me open with your beauty and visions. You are all brilliant. Many blessings on your journeys. To Charlie Parker, Seth Bernard, Galen Fulford and Seth Braun.

For the courageous readers and guides of the first manuscript: Mary McHenry, Peggy and Ted Warren, Tom Daly, Larry Tassiday—thank you for the faith and inspiration. And to the final readers: Richard Simonelli, Sharon Ferguson and Nancy Jane, thank you!

Last but not least my co-writer and editor James Churches and his kiva, the Moonbellies. He is truly a word and story weaver and bard. He knows this realm of the human mystery and of man's search for meaning.

Contents

Preface 1

Introduction 2

1 - Longing and Meaning 14

2 - Elders and Prayer 38

3 - To Believe—Prayer in Contemporary Life 62

4 - Shadow, Paradox, Projection 80

5 - Solitude and Nature 102

6 - Faith, Forgiveness, Reconciliation 124

7 - Emotion, Intuition, Ritual 140

8 - Simplicity 162

End Notes 179

Additional References 181

Further Reading 182

Preface

Seven years ago I began taking notes and collecting provocative poetry and stories of men, their questions about the purpose and meaning of their lives. After fifteen years of hearing thousands of men's stories a consistent theme emerged: men desire to be soulfully engaged in their lives, to live in passionate spiritual and heartful service to something larger, something that connects them to the essence of human nature.

It became apparent that many of us moderns felt a profound emptiness in our lives that could not be filled by more possessions, but could only be soothed by a certain kind of meaning. So often, under all of the discomfort, the inner and outer voices competing for attention, arose a simple age-old yearning to love and to serve the world in some heartful way. This book, more than anything, is an attempt to show some of the ways ordinary men have looked for and found meaning in their lives.

Writing this book has been a step along my own path to meaning, and has been served by the kindness of my friends and family. Four years ago James Churches came to me at a retreat and said he knew I was working on a book about men, their heart and soul lives. He offered his services to help get the book out into the world, himself being a dedicated writer and editor.

James became the mid-wife that helped this book be born, bringing the loose ends together into a manuscript that blended our styles. His soul life and mine are entwined in these pages, and in the lives of the beautiful men whose stories have been told. Thank you all and blessed be...

Jeffrey Duvall
Eldora, Colorado
Summer, 2001

Introduction

IT IS POSSIBLE, AND PERHAPS LIKELY, THAT THE VERY SOURCE OF human consciousness arose from a prayer, a communication with something greater. It may have gone something like this: an ancient man or woman has suffered a great loss, unable to place it or make sense of it, angry, desperate, frightened and trembling next to a small fire, no longer satisfied with the inherently timeless response of its animal mind, turns deep-set eyes toward the boundless night sky and asks that first halting human question: What…meaning…this? He runs the sharp edge of the bone scraper, given him by his grandfather, against the soft flesh of his palm, sees the old man demonstrating to him as a boy the uses of the tool, telling him stories of the hunt and the rituals of preparation, and all of this has brought him to this place, to this question of meaning.

I would not presume to enter this storm of human nature, this turbulent, deafening flood of hope and grief and mystery, and come out with answers. Thousands of theologians, philosophers and mystics have entered these waters with scholarship and discipline far greater than my own. These great masters have returned from the tempest with some picture of the storm, tried to place it in some objective form. Their contributions are of a kind much different from what I offer.

Mine is more along the lines of a shipwreck survivor, in awe of what he has witnessed and experienced, who combs the shores in search of remnants, bits and pieces of cargo, the leg of a chair, one edge of a picture frame, a wooden spoon, the hairs in a broken brush, the page of a journal, soggy and washed clean of ink, a feather from a hat, one broken shard of an old man's spectacles. From these relics of my own experience, I have accumulated a story about prayer. It is not a matter of interest to me that it be fact, that it stand up under logical scrutiny. It's possible that none of it is right. In the event that any of my scavenging touches you or provides something of value in your life, all the better. And should it be the opposite, that may be even more important. Often my deepest lessons have come from receiving what I don't want. I was told by many a guide and teacher to grasp from others what resonates for me and to let go what doesn't resonate. I invite you to do the same.

My story is the harvest from fifteen years of working with men in ritual settings. I have traveled to many places and sat in circles with thousands of people from all walks of life. What I have observed during this time is that men are hungry. I am hungry. We all have different tastes, and so what satisfies one man may hold no zest for another. Blessed be. Still, we share in common the hunger for meaning, fulfillment, a feeling of purpose, the knowledge that our lives matter. I've heard it said that God exists in the yearning. Maybe so. I don't know any more about this than anyone else. And I'm not interested in the intellectual debate about which approach to prayer is better than another. I don't want to leverage my view against another faith. Enough wars have been fought over such matters to discourage me from inciting conflict on the subject of prayer. Spiritual dead ends that leave us no alternative but to fight seem to contradict the soul's evolution. Rather, I seek ways to bring us together for the inquiry.

I desire to know: What is your path? Do you care for yourself, respect and hold yourself in enough love to find your personal path of heart? This is what matters to me. I don't care if it means sitting in church on Sundays, or sitting in meditation or a sweat lodge or a synagogue, mosque, cave or coven. We don't need to fight savagely about these things. The people and the earth have been devastated enough. Still, it is imperative that we continue the dialogue, while we keep our strong opinions held in loose gloves. It is possible to have fruitful, rewarding interactions without ever deciding one way is better or more correct than another.

One place of worship is not better than another. Mine is not *the* way. We need all the ways, all the approaches. In my travels, I have never found that one spiritual practice had more of a connection to meaning, spirit, ancestors and the soul than another. The beauty of the tundra comes from the linkage of many small systems. Some taking over others. Some able to hold on to only the harshest outcroppings of rock. Each interacting with and enriching the whole landscape, and thus each other. Hunters and the hunted. Do you agree that the moose, at times, needs the wolf to eat it?

There was a man once, a well respected elder in the peace movement, who was interviewed about his life. The interviewer suggested that he must feel good about his position as a pioneer in the peace movement, someone whom so many people had followed and emulated. He said, "No, not at all, I would have failed in my vision if anybody followed in my footsteps." His point was that for peace to work, individuals have to make it their own. Whatever the practice, the goal or desire, individuals are responsible and have the greatest impact by relating from their centers.

As difficult as it is at times, I mostly prefer to be in ceremonial and prayer circles with people who *are not* like minded. These times in which we live draw us to the difficult relationships with those we may dispute. Our souls call out for us to find ways to communicate and honor each other—at least to make the attempt a practice, and be willing to accept the outcome. In this way, our lives can enjoy a similar richness of diversity as that embodied by the tundra. Joseph Campbell told the story of his invitation to a prestigious conference on the state of human culture and consciousness in the late 20th Century. He was to speak to a group of the world's best minds. Campbell had recently quit his faculty post at a respected French university when he realized all he had done in his academic career was memorize other people's ideas and regurgitate them correctly. He didn't know what *he* thought, how his studies related to—as he would later become famous for saying—"follow your bliss." And so he came to this conference, prepared to speak about such matters, tingling with an intuition he was being set up.

He spoke the passion of his newfound awakening and awaited the response. The assembled experts shredded him, and it began to look as if he, invited to this important international conference, was a fool. The facilitator invited him to rebut. Campbell said an old South American shaman once told him that when you're climbing a steep mountain—

and that's what we're doing here, he emphasized—and a bird defecates on your head, do not release your grip to wipe it off! In other words, we have to remember what we're here for. We have to cultivate an inner strength, resources and allies, so we feel strong enough to engage at any level, so that when we are challenged, we have alternatives more noble than blind reprisal. It is the desperate man who responds to difficulty with violence, and furthers the stereotype that all men are violent. I do not believe this, even though we are born with the ability to kill—all of us, man, woman, child.

These capacities are native to the human condition and require attention, the skill of a disciplined heart. This is especially true for men, given recent discoveries of male brain structure. The findings indicate that evolution has tailored the brains of men to respond aggressively to the world around them. The attribute was continued, through natural selection, because it often made the difference in survival of the people. Given this as a natural propensity, it makes sense to work with it as a necessary and valuable force that can be embraced and refined in service of responsible living. A fundamental component of this refinement is to address soul hunger. This, I have found, leads to maturity. A man's trustworthiness compares to his knowledge of the inner terrain, the crooked bones and quagmires of our ancestors.

I had the pleasure of working with a 100-year-old healer in Chicago I knew as Dr. Herman. He was an incredibly well-traveled man, a friend of Mahatma Gandhi, and in whose presence I felt humble. On our first acquaintance, he asked me if I believe in God. Oh no, I thought, here we go. I knew he was a devout Christian. I'm not going to believe in the *right* God, I thought, and he's going to reject and shame me. I told him I believe in nature. "Good," he said, "as long as you believe." That's what mattered to him. That's what he needed to know to take me as a student. I would offer the same question to you. What do you believe in? What do you have faith in? Upon what do you draw upon in hard times? To what do you express gratitude in good times? And are you capable of gratitude and growth from the hard times? Where is it in your life that you contact the sacred? This is how poet Mary Oliver works with these same questions:

I don't know exactly what prayer is.
I do know how to pay attention, how to fall down
into the grass, how to kneel down in the grass,
how to be idle and blessed, how to stroll through the fields,
which is what I have been doing all day.
Tell me, what else should I have done?
Doesn't everything die at last, and too soon?
Tell me, what is it you plan to do
with your one wild and precious life?[1]

I do not raise these questions as abstract points for discussion. To me, there is urgency in this. The children cry out for their elders to know this terrain and to guide them into it. How many prisons are we going to construct in order to lock away the dangerous, anti-social young men lost in Dante's dark woods and with no beacon? What does it say about us as a culture that we have little ability to relate to the wild aggression of our adolescent men? When will we stop lying to ourselves and our children about who we really are and learn to look our sons and daughters in the eyes and tell them we know they have the power to kill, that we know this destructive tapestry within ourselves, and we know of alternatives? Michael Meade has said the soul is like iron that needs to be hammered out in life. As adults we must learn about this hammering, practice it and utilize our life's experience as the blows that pound out our inner dimension, and become aware of what stops us from knowing this natural and necessary process. Rainer Marie Rilke speaks about such things in his *Letters to a Young Poet*:

> ...and I want to beg you, as much as I can, to be patient toward all that is unresolved in your heart and try to love *the questions them-selves,* like locked rooms and like books written in a very foreign tongue. Do not now seek the answers, that cannot be given you because you would not be able to live them. And the point is to live everything. *Live* the questions now. Perhaps you will then gradually, without noticing it, live along some distant day into the answer.[2]

Victor Frankl describes his experience standing before a firing squad, watching the soldiers enact the protocol and ritual of execution, and at the final moment, the only thing remaining the command to "fire!", a bomb drops behind them, and the soldiers scatter and his life is saved. In that moment, the moment just before death, Frankl found the deepest serenity of his life. He describes the moment in his book *Man's Search for Meaning*:

> In a position of utter desolation, when man cannot express himself
> in a positive action, when his only achievement may consist in
> enduring his suffering in the right way—in an honorable way—in
> such a position man can, through loving contemplation of the
> image he carries of his beloved, achieve fulfillment.[3]

All too often in our time, the moments of utter desolation are responded to with violence, either on ourselves or on others. Young people and adults alike recoil from difficulty and suffering because they do not know, or have never been around somebody who knows, the fulfillment and grace described by Victor Frankl. I don't want to set people's agendas for how they approach these dark and frightening places within themselves. My interest is to point out the depth of human potential for inspired living. I only hope, in some small way, to call people to the threshold, to perhaps highlight the gateway, provide some encouragement, stories and bits and pieces of gathered inspiration that may serve as a torch to light the way at least for a short distance, and maybe, if fortune smiles, to help my brothers and sisters find the sanctuary within themselves that houses their faith. This alone will carry them forward when my small torch burns out.

I have been interested for many years in various healing practices and shamanic rituals, known by my ancestors and healers around the world. A common truth I have found among them all is that without faith, little can come into us that sustains the heart, soul and community. We all have the capacity to block out what we need so dearly by our own skepticism and doubt. So many of us have been subjected to oppressive approaches to faith that we have learned not to trust and have been left with so little. Men in particular have been blamed for the ills of the world and have learned to distrust each other, themselves and their gods. This type of training for men in our culture fractures our connections in the continuum of existence. In the ways that we are separated from our own greatness, the potential of our godliness, our divinity, there is the possibility of blindly harming others, the spirit of nature, the delicate balance of evolution and growth in our souls and that of the community. The path of blame and scorn only drives the wedge deeper into a man's heart.

The blind finger pointing does not make men stronger or more loving or more trustworthy. Rather, why not all of us own the mistakes of our heritage? Why not all of us embrace the tragedies our people lived through and in so doing sanctify the journey and pledge to do better ourselves? Prayer can help with this. I'm interested in helping people find something, anything, that works for them and gives them access to the universal language of prayer, its one face with many faces. I'm interested in the simple act of prayer, of listening, of attention to our own indigenous wisdom, to the exploration and continuance of what the human soul already knows, to the practice of attending the nonlinear truths as guiding forces and to challenge the dominant, logical, linear-based systems and practicalities. And to know the difference.

I remember an Episcopal bishop who noticed me waiting on tables in Marquette, Michigan, and invited me to his home. He brought me to this intimidating mansion the church provided and into a library stacked from floor to ceiling with volumes of books. He pointed to them and told me he didn't need any of these books, that none of them brought him any closer to God—outer or the inner, and perhaps more germane, the lack of separation between the two. And then he reached up and pulled one small volume, and handed it to me. "But this one," he said, "this is the one of them all." And he gave me that book, *The Lives of a Cell*,[4] by Lewis Thomas. I was shocked. Me, a waiter, a lowly peasant, but this high holy man in the church saw me. He *saw* me. And he became a mentor and guide and inspired me to find my own faith, to simply learn to believe in myself. He knew that the important thing was not in any particular dogma, but in the personal inspiration.

This is a serious issue for me. Too many times have I heard stories of men shamed and oppressed by autocratic religious approaches. I myself come from the Catholic faith. I am still transported by the smell of frankincense and ringing bells to my time as an altar boy. To this day I have a deep respect and love for the church. Still, I see in it the potential to shut down the creative expression of the individual soul. All doctrines have a shadow—as my words most surely do as well—and in the unacknowledged shadow lies the potential for abuse. To me, the abusiveness comes from power and hierarchy that is set up as superior to the individual and discounts and in some cases condemns our instinctive knowing. The faithful either bow to this power or risk exile and even annihilation. Hawthorne's *Scarlet Letter* speaks to this, but history has no shortage of examples, from the Spanish Inquisition to the Salem witch trials, to the modern cults of Branch Davidians and the Jonestown massacre. These are cases in which logic and intellect and the rigid human constructs of political expediency crush the deeper truths each of us holds. I believe that our warm hearts know our soul's lineage. Our ancestors' lives, their experience, let's call it wisdom, is our very blood's knowing. I like the way the Lakota medicine man Frank Fools Crow put it in the book by Thomas E. Mails when describing the conversion of his people to Christianity:

> We Sioux prayed to *Wakan-Tanka* personally and constantly. We even thanked him for the lessons that hardship taught us… So both the good times and the bad times taught us valuable lessons about life and about daily prayer. What confused me most was the fact that the churches had books with prayers already written in them by white people who had lived a long time ago, that these were the only ones we Indians were to say as members and even then only inside the building that was called the church. I couldn't figure out how prayers like that could fit our daily needs. They weren't personal enough.[5]

Didn't the Lakota people have a sophisticated spiritual tradition just as vital, just as valid and worthy as that of the European settlers? How easy would it have been to find a common ground had the new immigrants to the Great Plains learned that the Lakota people believed in a trinity of father, son and holy spirit very similar to theirs? That said, it should be noted Fools Crow was a practicing Roman Catholic his entire life, went to church regularly and took communion, yet he continued to practice the traditional Lakota healing ceremonies of sweat lodge and Yuwipi. How did he reconcile these apparently contradictory approaches? This is what I'm trying to get at. I don't want to blame Christianity or set up another us-and-them polarity. Any faith, any practice, any method can become oppressive and harmful. Some of the New Age ideals are terribly restrictive in my judgment. It's easy enough to go astray. What I'm hoping for is a coming together, a free and open dialogue based on mutual respect. I envision an expansive practice of ritual, a rich, diverse life of prayer, openness for healing, responsible actions toward the earth, each other and our inner selves. I believe the earth and our ancestors call us to this. With what seems to be less and less connection with solitude and introspective practices, and a world more and more degraded, this call I speak of here, expressed by many an elder, demands to be heard.

In prayer, we can show we are listening. Prayer can serve as a gateway to the dimension between night and day, between life and death. It can and does serve us in the quest for peace, but we have to slow down long enough and make room in ourselves for it to enter. Again, the ways to do this are too many to count. Larry Dossey[6] has exhaustively researched the phenomena of prayer. He found that the context did not matter. The style, method, words—none of it seemed to affect the outcome. The act itself, the sincerity and intention, were the common factors in effective prayer. When I say effective, I'm not talking about getting results, in the concrete sense of asking for something and receiving it directly. The power of prayer is not about taking away the pain of the world. To me it's about personal evolution connected to all that has been and will be, about being able to hear and receive the blessings and support already waiting to be given. An elder at Spirit Camp, a men's retreat held in the ceremonial hands of ritual and prayer, once said that ritual becomes belief. What you pray for, you become. There's that old prayer adage, "Be careful what you ask for." This may appear trite, but its simple message calls us to the mystery of prayer. I've spoken with hundreds, perhaps thousands of men, about prayer and ritual, participated in ceremony with them, married and buried them, and almost to a man they concede an inability to control the outcome. To let oneself be guided, to trust and have faith in one's own divine grace is one of the great gifts of prayer. And in such surrender comes unimaginable possibility, the room and space inside for personal growth and evolution. The greatly respected therapist Milton Ericson knew about this. He let the patient structure the treatment and said, "I always trust my unconscious." He let himself be guided by something beyond his ordinary awareness. All of us can tap into this resource, and in so doing, serve ourselves and our communities in simple, profound ways.

I invite you to join me on this exploration of prayer, to take any bits or parts that serve you on your journey, and pay attention and trust your own sense of what doesn't fit for you. As I said before, I don't presume to have answers about this subject, just some experience, some stories, some gathered artifacts that, under ideal circumstances, may provide a little guidance, a signpost or two as to some possible topography. Our elders and nature teach us that life's main chore is to plumb the depths of our full potential in heart, soul and meaning. Each of us has our distinct way of being, healing, growing and expressing beauty. I offer this book as a prayer, as a gratitude to my ancestors, with the hope that it can serve and contribute to the richness of life. I am reminded of the gift given us by Sir Laurens van der Post in his documentaries on the Bushmen of the Kalahari[7]. After a long search for an active, functioning Bushmen clan, van der Post and his colleagues finally came upon a solitary, traditional Bushman in the desert. The guide, who came from a tribe of Bushmen no longer living the nomadic life, nonetheless knew the native tongue and spoke the words to his nomadic brother that caused him to run toward him as if something terrible had happened. When asked what he said, the guide told van der Post he had said to his brother he was hungry. Sir Laurens thought it remarkable that the wild and free Bushman would respond to a call of hunger with such urgency. The guide informed him he had told his brother he had "the big hunger," the one that is beyond the stomach's demand for food, but comes from the heart's cry for meaning. This made perfect sense to van der Post, and he later said, "...once what you are living and what you are doing has for you meaning, it is irrelevant whether you are happy or unhappy. You are content. You're not alone in your spirit. You belong." And so I offer this book as a possible tool in finding your belonging in the beauty of your soul. Bless the big hunger in all of us, and bless the heart's knowing of just how urgent the hunger is, and may it be so that when we recognize the big hunger in ourselves, in our brothers, sisters and children, we run to it and do not shy from it or recoil but run to it and find some way to soothe it, that we arrive together at the many gates of initiation, our growing into who we are, a little bit hungry.

It is helpful, I find, to come into our passages with a belly less than full. It seems to help us notice the unexpected blessings, and necessary challenges, life brings to us. A hungry heart and soul notices the basic simple truths coming to us from our ancestors, rendered in life's meaning. It is normal, and often less impressive, to know the natural power of kindness, compassion and love toward ourselves and others. I offer this wayfarer's story as inspiration to find our purpose and let it be our guide. My offering, and prayer, is that we can be active in our families, communities, and be the makers of human evolution. I ask that we not surrender to the many reasons and forces in our culture, in our psyches, that confuse our own integrity. May this small gift be a tribute to our ancestors and to all of nature, past, present and future. In this spirit I dedicate these simple thoughts.

1 Longing and Meaning

I'VE HEARD IT SAID THE GREAT LIFE OFTEN LACKS GLAMOUR AND MAY be poor in the trappings of material success. Another source of richness offers itself. It is an intangible wealth, whose treasures lie in the store-house of mystery. Sometimes difficult to see, or touch with the hands, these riches offer true substance and grounding for the soul. For many, prayer is a way to discover themselves and their own paths in life. It often requires an orientation towards acceptance, to bathe in the depth and chaos of giving up control and surrendering to a life of service. It may appear as a contradiction, but such a practice can ground one in personal responsibility and strength, a life pathway not so much based on accomplishing the goals but on openness to mystery sustained by a deep longing for meaning and purpose. I have seen the richness of heart in these ways among many people I've known. They seem to live more in the flux and ebb of community and natural rhythms. Their lives become a long series of passages experienced in the dedicated practice of acceptance and connection.

It is said the Mohican people of the northeastern Americas speak of prayer as the sacred container of each full day and cycle. The practice is to greet the rising sun with prayers for guidance and the courage to do Great Spirit's work this day. At sundown, thanksgiving prayers are offered, for another day of living, for the white tail deer that will feed the clan for the coming weeks, for the births and deaths, the joys and sorrows that came through another day of living in the miracle of being. In such a practice, a man makes room in his heart for meaning to enter. He empties his expectations and the notion of having it his way. He does not give up his longing, his desire for a good life. Rather he drinks from the longing as a continual spring that rises from his soul. Prayer connects him to this place, and the meaning he finds there grows out of him and nourishes others.

I often suggest to the men I work with that we begin by inhaling the wholeness of the vital air, the trees, the rocks, the waters that surround us. Take it in deeply and experience it filling us completely. On the exhale, breath out any expectations. Feel the pressure to perform, to accomplish, to achieve, deflate and dissipate with the exhale. This emptying piece is so essential. Without it, there is no room for the primary body and blood messages to enter. Meaning is locked out by the incessant prodding to get something done, our pervasive cultural imperative. The spirit and soul dimensions are suffocated by these pressures as native plants might be by rolls of Kentucky bluegrass sod.

With this opening in place, I sometimes ask men what has been the greatest learning experience in their lives. I ask them how this inspires and informs them now. It may come as a surprise to you that the greatest teaching was often, on the surface, a failure. It wasn't what they thought they had wanted. It went contrary to their opinion of how it should have been, or what they had been led to believe was right. But underneath these opinions, through the gift of an unexpected teaching, men find their passion. They find the sources of their self worth and knowing that calls them to live their lives fully, perhaps differently than they may have wanted, but most importantly, to live passionately.

The purpose of these questions is not to lead men in any particular direction. It is more important to encourage others to take the risk to discover passion and inspiration toward a path with heart. Ezra Pound said, "The only thing that endures is emotion." Too much is lost when prayer and ritual—the invitation to spirit, to blood, the ancestral line, our own urgent longings—are neglected. So to me, prayer is in many ways a gateway, as it was for the Mohican man, through which our yearning can pass and bring vitality to our every action.

Many years ago, my friend, colleague and teacher Tom Daly, invited me into a spiritual practice. I remember arriving at night into an old Denver neighborhood, where tall elm still watched over the parked cars and porches. It looked like an old templelike structure, tall and skinny, a spire. I was greeted at the door by Tom and some other men who showed me where to place my belongings. Soon after, I was welcomed down two steps through a doorway that had been covered by a colorful blanket. The deep reverberation of a heartbeat drum had been there from the moment I walked up to the structure. Once past the blanket, I recognized the source of that primal rhythm in a large drum standing in a corner. The room was almost dark, but I could make out the shadows of indistinguishable bodies moving in the space. The ceiling was so tall and the room so dark, it seemed to have no boundaries. The room was thick with a sense of reverence, something I hadn't felt since my days as an altar boy in the old cathedrals of my youth. Some of the men among the twenty-five were whispering among each other, with occasional quiet laughter. Others were kneeling in front of what appeared to be altars, laid out in the cardinal directions of a compass. Each altar was covered with a cloth, laid with candles and powerful objects like carved heartshapes, hunting knives, effigies to what appeared a variety of religious symbols. There was something familiar in the candles and the objects that seemed to encapsulate much of what symbolized humanity and manhood. I began to realize the room was much taller than it was long or wide. The walls were draped with clothes and a series of masks that represented many of the emotional and spiritual aspects of human longing. Mixed in with the candles was a strong smell of incense, some of it exotic, like copal, some like the scent of pine bows burning. Time began to play tricks with me. I sensed in my body a certain knowing, even closeness, to this way, even though I had never experienced it in my current life. Tom and some of his helpers called us together to share what they were calling an orientation meeting. They guided us through an old spiritual practice he and the others had inherited from a southern New Mexico medicine woman. We circled into a meditative walk. The power of the large wooden and leather drum began to fill out the room with more intensity. The beat grew faster. From there we stepped into a ritual journey that lasted for hours. It ended in a similar manner as it had begun, with the drum slowing to the original heartbeat. In the silence, I experienced in a profoundly new way, a connection with my blood and the inheritance of my own ancestry. There was some kind of non-logical remembering, as if I had come home. I had somehow been wandering for thirty years and had at last found a home. The newness of the home was that no central figure was worshipped. There was no separation from any of the ways. It was as if I were a stone that had been tumbled down a stream, with all the edges worn smooth, and was eventually deposited in a still pond. It was the beginning of my settling into that sandy bottom, washed over by the four seasons, finding a place of belonging. And aware of the coming floods and droughts that will sweep it into the next transformation.

This form I experienced—was initiated into—brought me to myself, to an understanding of some truth about who I am that I had suspected, but not known deeply. It brought me to a truth about the inner world, and how important it is to continually return to the core. What I've learned from these gatherings is that the work may often be that of a hard-rock miner who heaves a rusty pick at an old stone. Prayer, or quiet contemplation, a kind of openness, is a way to sharpen the blade of the pick, and subtly, to direct the blows at the soft places or the cracks and fissures in the rock, and perhaps, in some alchemical way, to alter the composition of the stone, to make it softer, more pliant, less rigid. If nothing else it can be a light to show the way, to make conscious the actions of this inner working. The point is to go there. We must find ways to reach our primal energy. As Thoreau said, "The only thing of importance is wildness."[8] Yet, in general, as a culture many of us have been separated from primal wildness, the passionate beauty that is life, that is our birthright. It concerns me that we may lose this essence, and yet to reclaim it is fraught with risk and danger. That is why I pray and suggest so strongly to others the development of their own practice. Who can approach these dark and turbulent waters in isolation? Who can reclaim his power, his primary or archetypal virility without allies, guardians and guides? Without his spirit and soul and body team, his totems and ancestral lineage? Prayer is a way to assemble the support, to galvanize the will and marshal the courage to embark. And to embark I say is human destiny.

One way to begin and to continue is to find some inspiration in nature (that includes human nature). I have sat in a canoe on a Minnesota lake and watched a solitary loon lift its throat and roll back its tongue and offer its haunting call to the first rays of dawn, low and lonely mingled with the rising mist that welcomes grief and beauty at once to the creatures of the lake. As I am there in the presence, I too receive the blessing, I too receive the dawn and come to life in the slow difficult way the new day is born out of darkness. I experience myself as larger than I can contain, larger than my concept of who I am or who I was told I am or who I was supposed to be in order to fit in and be compliant. Here, on the lake, with the loon and the mist, the still, ancient trees, the moss, snails, worms, salamanders and pike, I know myself as a coming sun, an eternal longing, a part of some vast miracle, and I am humbled and grateful. Each of us in our own way connects to a sense of greater self, wherever we are. Nature, even in the city, thrives in the cooing pigeons, plays in the feisty squirrels, and calls out to us in the gulls that circle our landfills. Everywhere it is possible to know the simple connection, at times, and it is enough then and always, by doing nothing more than listening, to hear, as one elder puts it, with the ears of the heart, in itself a prayer.

One year I brought a group of men to Negro Bill Canyon near Moab, Utah, for a three-day fast. They were out when the storm came in. Two days earlier we had walked nearly five miles into the canyon and had completed a day of council and preparation, considering safety and confirming the questions and prayers they would take into their solos. They had been out one night. One man had camped near the base of a 220-foot crevice in the Navaho red sandstone painted with the clearest representations of Kokopelli I'd ever seen, complete with erect penises, as was the old way, a row of them painted around a bend in the rock. The man camped and played his bamboo flute in harmony with the trickster god. Another man was at the base of the canyon and another farther out. A storm flew up the canyon, furious with lightning and thunder and rain. You could tell by the way it came in and dropped that is was serious. The lightning actually sparked horizontally down the canyon and bounced off of the walls like a ricocheting bullet. One naturally begins to think less about the details or worries of one's life and focuses on survival. It was a flash flood area. I had known a man caught in a flash flood in the same canyon. It rained into the night. Toward midnight it intensified to the point of being beyond endurance, with explosive thunder and blinding lightning. I was camped under an open tarp with a center pole. The water was starting to flow down where I was; it was spewing over the edges of the canyon in sheets in a thrashing, screaming storm, the kind of ruckus where you don't know if a wave of water will wash you away. In the middle of all this, I heard this tapping on the tarp. One of the men had returned with a look of terror on his face. He was embarrassed but wanted to come in with me. A while later another scratched on the tarp, and he came in with his gear. They came back in shock. They thought they were going to die. None of them had been in a storm like this. The third man never came in, and we imagined him swept away. In these times of chaos that can hit us like a furious storm or can hit us on a Monday morning while driving to work, the one healing salve is devotion, to each other and the storm of the very existence we share.

The storm shook their whole psyches loose. The passion and wildness of nature met their passionate souls, as if to say, "Hey! Wake up!" They were a basket of laundry, shook up, wrung out and cleansed by the power of the storm. The fuzz that sets in from the comfort of our modern age, the cares of money, sex, status, were all washed away. They walked out differently than they walked in. The walk in was difficult, but the walk out was like cutting the distance by two thirds. They had found something old and true about themselves that night when they were all out praying for their lives, under one of those sandstone faces that could have broken off and crushed them or been the source of a deluge. The experience brought to these men in one night what years of study and training could not have given them, a degree of patience and compassion for their people and respect for the power of nature, less concern for the contemporary cultural magnetism that doesn't necessarily breed this kind of awareness. This happened in an instant. Nature brought the challenge. Prayer showed the way. Transformation came. This is one of the ways, an example of a journey.

The third man did come in the next day, his eyes ablaze with his deepest beauty, his wild nature. He had come to terms with the possibility he might die out there. And yet he stayed, knowing that he would learn something about how to live. Hearing his story we all realized his courage and endurance had been a great prayer.

In some ways, these men came there to have their hearts broken open. Nature, the power and beauty and awe of it, can break us open and bring us to the place of receiving blessings. Alice Walker[9] has spoken of the ways in which her heart has been broken open and spilled feelings, opened so the wind may pass through it. What does it take for us to find a path that opens us in this way? How do we place ourselves in the path of an overwhelming storm, so that we are driven to the very bedrock of our souls and this too breaks open and we are swept into the grief of life? When we can feel and be alive fully? Michael Meade[10] talks about the value of betrayal, when the youthful innocence that trusts that all will be perfect for us gets wounded. I see that each season must be betrayed by the one that comes after it, and so the cycles may continue. The ongoing disappointment, the loss of expectations, the ability, as the poet Rilke says, "To be defeated, decisively by greater and greater opponents," are the ways in which awakening can touch us. To play safe and only spend time with "like minded people" can cut out the diversity that enriches the greatest of teachings. These teachings can only come from reaching for what we most desire and not getting it, or having it so briefly the pain of not being able to get back nearly kills us—there lives meaning.

When I was a young man living outside of Detroit in Monroe, Michigan, I worked in an automobile plant—a Ford stamping plant, steel parts, bumpers, wheels, big coil springs—and I stood at a bumper stamping machine for twelve hours a day, twenty-one straight days at one stretch. After work we'd go right to the bar in an attempt to balance the numbness with alcohol; then I'd go home to my grandparents and sleep and get up and do it again. Standing at that machine, I'd go into a sort of trance, surrounded by this constant explosion of steel against steel, whistles, these big, old fashioned metal fans blowing and the temperature a hundred and twenty degrees. Trying to have some kind of a life, it was like I turned into a machine myself, caught in a limbo, being stamped out into a form from which there was no escape. There were thousands of bumpers stored out back rusting, and yet here we were inside, stamping out new ones. These were bumpers that had become obsolete, because new bumpers had to be able to absorb a five-mile-per-hour impact, and so they were stacked fifty feet high, covering four or five acres.

I remember standing there as a young man wondering if this was it, the reason I was born, to serve this false god of industry and money. Every week when the foreman would come up and give us our checks, there was a moment of satisfaction, as if some father-like god figure approved of what you had done. But then driving out, we were stopped and searched in case we had stolen something, like a glob of copper or a pair of nice leather gloves, and the momentary satisfaction disappeared. We'd go to the bar to try to find some meaning, some laughter, camaraderie, or maybe sex, but were never quite fulfilled by it. I died there as a boy in that factory, slowly, day-by-day my soul crushed in a hot metal press. Leaving that factory, having arrived before the sun rose, walking out with the sun already set, never having known the light of day, I was capable of committing horrors in the world. I look back on it and can appreciate the metaphor. It's as if this industrial age continues to stamp out men in a form that doesn't serve them or the culture, but the machines can't change. They continue to stamp out men in the shape to which their dies are cast. Rainer Maria Rilke speaks of these things in this poem, translated by Robert Bly:

> The kings of the world are growing old
> and they shall have no inheritors.
> Their sons died when they were boys,
> and their starving exhausted daughters
> abandoned the sick crown to the mob.
> The mob broke the crown into tiny bits of gold,
> and the lord of the world, the master of the age,
> melts the bits in fires down to machines.
> The machines do his orders with low growls
> for joy is not on their side.
> The ore itself feels homesick
> it wants to abandon the minting houses

and wheels that offer it such a meager life
And out of the factory and payroll boxes it wants
to go back into the veins of thrown open mountains
which will close again behind it. [11]

I too yearned, though I didn't know it, to return to the veins of thrown open mountains, and in time did do that and found my soul. I would, however, hasten to remember that I am not separate from or superior to that factory or those men who gave their lives to the machine so that their families could be clothed, sheltered and fed. What choice did most of them have? Were they not stamped out in a form to fit the machine, stiff and mechanical in the way they operate the levers and switches of their positions on the line? Were they not raised to be good obedient boys and do as they are told? And do they not drive on their short vacations to Lake Superior in the same cars for which they stamp out the parts? Am I superior to them? And if I want to imagine myself above, then what do I do about my use of the automobile? Can I honestly protest against Exxon for spilling oil on the pristine Alaskan coast when I drive to the funeral of a dear friend in Kansas because I want to pay tribute to her beautiful life? This is why it's so hard, why I am so consumed with grief, a profound sadness for the way things are and what we have lost, and yet I am a co-creator of the mess. How can I hold this? How can any of us stand up and claim to contain ourselves, let alone the totality of creation? Yet somehow, in some humble, human way, our souls call us to the responsibility. And we answer in the ways we find available to us. The Zen master Thich Nhat Hanh describes the journey in a poem *Please Call Me By My True Name*:

Do not say that I'll depart tomorrow
because even today I still arrive.

Look deeply: I arrive in every second
to be a bud on a spring branch,
to be a tiny bird, with wings still fragile,
learning to sing in my new nest,

to be a caterpillar in the heart of a flower,
to be a jewel hiding itself in a stone.

I still arrive, in order to laugh and to cry,
in order to fear and to hope,
the rhythm of my heart is the birth and
death of all that are alive.

I am the mayfly metamorphosing on the
surface of the river,
and I am the bird which, when spring comes,
arrives in time to eat the mayfly.

I am the frog swimming happily in the
clear water of a pond,
and I am also the grass snake who,
approaching in silence,
feeds itself on the frog.

I am the child in Uganda, all skin and bones,
my legs as thin as bamboo sticks,
and I am the arms merchant, selling deadly
weapons to Uganda.

I am the 12-year-old girl refugee
on a small boat,
who throws herself into the ocean after
being raped by a sea pirate,
and I am the pirate, my heart not yet capable
of seeing and loving.

I am a member of the politburo, with
plenty of power in my hands, and I am the man who has to pay his
"debt of blood" to my people,
dying slowly in a forced labor camp.

My joy is like the spring, so warm it makes
flowers bloom in all walks of life.
My pain is like a river of tears, so full it
fills up the four oceans.

Please call me by my true names,
so I can hear all my cries and my laughs
at once,
so I can see that my joy and pain are one.

Please call me by my true names,
so I can wake up,
and so the door of my heart can be left open,
the door of compassion. [12]

I wish there were a way to insert silence at these times…

When poems are read at gatherings, we usually hold the silence, and
in this way the words and feelings and images can penetrate to the deepest places in us, and touch, as Master Hanh says, "a jewel hiding itself
in a stone." In this spirit I would suggest that in reading this book, or
any other, take moments away from the text, consider and contemplate
passages that inspire or bemuse you. I have found over the years that the
soul works much slower than the mind. What the mind can comprehend instantly may take the soul minutes, hours, days longer, and sometimes years later a poem or experience revisits us, as if held in an oak bar-
rel and allowed to ferment until the time we can appreciate the true flavor. My counsel here is simply do not rush. Our world seems to me so
charged with pressure, something always pushing us the way automobile
drivers ride our tails as we travel down freeways. Productivity and accomplishment dominate our value systems and in their domineering way
leave little room for the nuance and subtlety of the inner life. And so…

Returning for a moment to the stories of Utah's red sandstone
canyons and the automobile factory of Detroit, the polar opposites of

these stories represent the hands of a human body. The left way over here and the right way over there. When we bring them together to clasp at our hearts in an act of prayer, this unity forms a conduit through which the prayer may travel. I might prefer one side over the other, but as a dear elder has said, "We are crucified by our preferences." By bringing them together in the sort of responsible attentiveness described in Master Hanh's poem, a third possibility is created. It is this new possibility that interests me. How do we create for ourselves new possibilities out of apparent hopelessness? What about the millions of men who are trapped in glass and steel towers sixty hours a week? Are they to be shunned? Is there no hope for them? Or are their third and fourth possibilities? David Whyte, in his book *The Heart Aroused*,[13] writes beautifully of the path with heart in corporate life. There are ways, always, to find meaning. It is time to stop blaming and judging the modern world. It is our world and we are all responsible for it. Even the worst of atrocities are ours: the genocide in Rowanda, the ethnic cleansing in Bosnia, the insanity in Cambodia, the gang killings in Los Angeles, the Oklahoma City bombing, Columbine High School massacre, and the World Trade Center and Pentagon attacks. I don't claim to understand these things, but I feel them, I open myself to the grief in them, and I believe if more of us did so, a third or fourth possibility might emerge. This is what interests me. Sitting around at a cocktail party bemoaning the brutality of the world, and often blaming men and the destructive patriarchy for everything that's wrong, does not capture my attention. In fact, I would suggest that such behavior actually feeds the very things we see as so horrible. To heal them, the hands come together, from their opposed sides, and clasp at the heart in prayer.

When I first came to Boulder, Colorado, I worked with a medicine man, an authentic healer, whose favorite question was, "What stops you?" I've interpreted this question many ways over the years. One way I frame the questions, or expand it, is, "How do I keep myself from the meaning of my life?" Or, "What prevents me from being fully who I am?" These questions can be prayers and one can sit with a rattle or next to a favorite tree in the biggest most crowded city in the world and hold the question, "What stops me?" I find that again and again, my judgments and opinions get in the way of meaning and purpose.

I was told as a freshman in high school by one of the Fathers of Verona that I would be in prison by the time I was twenty-one. My mother recently sent me a box of my old things, and in it was a two page document compiled by that priest listing all of the things that were wrong with me. He claimed I was selfish and insensitive to others, that all I seemed to think about was having fun and that I was dangerous and angry. In many ways he was speaking truth. I can remember being so crazy because everybody was always telling me, "You've got to change, you've got to change." But nobody told me how, nobody showed me a way. They just pointed out what was wrong with me. I wish someone would have read me this poem by Anthony De Mello:

I was a neurotic for years. I was anxious and depressed
and selfish. Everyone kept telling me to change.

I resented them, and I agreed with them, and I wanted to
change…but simply couldn't…no matter how hard I tried.

What hurt the most was that, like the others, my best
friend (my wife/husband) kept insisting that I change.
So I felt powerless and trapped.

Then one day, my friend said to me, "Don't change. I
love you just as you are."

These words were music to my ears. "Don't change.
Don't change. Don't change…I love you just as you are."

I relaxed. I came alive. And suddenly…I changed!

Now I know that I couldn't really change until I found
someone who would love me whether I change or not. [14]

When I was a young man, most people did not seem to appreciate the concept expressed here by De Mello. I remember becoming profoundly angry because I really did want a better life, but instead of receiving guidance, I generally was condemned. People could only see the problem and point judgmental fingers at me. Did this help me change? It had about as much effect as the cocktail party complainers do on whatever situation they find reprehensible. And again, as I said earlier, their complaints and criticisms drew me even more to the very problems they told me I had to change. Looking through that box of memories my mother sent, it is still vivid to me how desolate I felt at that time, so lost, and in some ways taken over by the dark side. I got the attitude that if I'm going to go down in this storm, I'm going to drag a few people down with me. I would make my mark making other people's lives miserable. It was the only way I could get attention, a twisted attempt to be initiated. A lot of my buddies didn't make it. They were killed in cars or motorcycles or bars. Where were the elders who knew the way across the water? In my rage I could not see them.

I want to acknowledge here something that may be vexing or confusing to readers. Themes may appear to contradict one another. It may seem as if I am saying the opposite of what has previously been asserted. I don't see any way around this. There's a Walt Whitman poem about this later that elaborates the theme. What is true in one instance is not true in the next. The context changes the truth, and the nature of the soul terrain is a vastness that can hold tremendous diversity. What is true for you may not be true for me. What is true for me one day— the day perhaps I hear a dear friend has cancer or that the car repair is going to cost a few thousand more than anticipated—may not be true the next, and so on. At times, for example, I feel overwhelmed with sadness at what feels like a vacuum of meaning in of our culture. It can feel as if we have completely abandoned the ways of the ancestors. Then, in a sort of epiphany, I can see that it is all okay and as it should be. I can own the shadows, accept the difficulties and carry on with my vision of how it can be, and keep my hand in the wave of destiny. So be it.

Returning to the question, then, of where are the elders? I can recognize that, in truth, they were there for me as a boy. They floated down the River Raisin every spring in the form of driftwood bobbing in the waves and currents of the brown and swollen river. My friends and I would fish them out and build ourselves a hut, attached to the living willow tree in our backyard, a huge grandmother with an eight foot trunk and a canopy of drooping branches large enough to shade a small army of boys. We built our hut there every spring from the old wood that floated down the stream. These elders gave us sanctuary from the troubles in our lives. And in the fall, we took apart the hut and sent the elders downstream to serve those next in line. Somehow we knew, and nature knew, what we needed, and it floated to us. We intuitively knew enough to fish it out and build with it, despite everything that was going wrong around us.

I truly believe that those who attempted to help me by their judgments had good intentions and wanted what they imagined were good things for me. I see now it was the context that was off. It would be tempting for me to do the very thing with these experiences that I have made a case against. And so to maintain integrity, I continually bless and embrace the difficulties that I grew up with. This is the way through. Our parents were the cannon fodder for the modern age. We're standing on their broken bones and broken hearts. I'm thankful for their sacrifices and to be able now to see alternatives. If I were to remain stuck in feeling victimized by the way I was treated, there would be no way out and I would have no choice but to live as a victim or a perpetrator. Instead, let us bring the opposites together and be open to the mystery of what may come. There's an old classic of the hippie days that speaks to these ideas. Thaddeus Golas' *Lazy Man's Guide to Enlightenment* says:

> What you cannot think about, you cannot control. What you cannot conceive of in your awareness, you will stumble over in your path. Violent human beings are precisely those who refuse at some time to conceive that they could be violent. It also happens that if you are unwilling to conceive of people being victims of violence, you may become a victim yourself, for you will not be sufficiently aware of how it happens to avoid it. Everything that is manifest begins in the spirit: every evil that is manifest to us is there because

we refused to conceive of causing it, or denied someone else the freedom to conceive of it. The way out, as hard as it may be to believe, is not by resisting further, by moving the furniture around, but by being willing to conceive of it—by loving it, in short. As we should have done in the first place.[15]

Rather than be encouraged to find my meaning, to learn how to love my dangerous aspects, I was taught—and this indoctrination is shared by so many of the men I have worked with—how to hate myself. The teaching focused often on my passion and worked to suppress it. Many of my teachers, religious mentors, and the community in general worked as if they were all following the same blueprint to eliminate my wildness. It all came from an innocent and inherited repressive culture, a fear that if these masculine powers were not suppressed they would destroy all that is good. I don't believe anyone intended to hurt me, but nonetheless, the message was clear, or at least my interpretation of it was clear: there is something wrong with you, the way you are is not acceptable. I felt doomed to carry on my life from this place, to live a sort of half life devoid of passion, purpose and meaning. I would compete for power by trying to be attractive, wealthy and a falsely cool guy. I would devote myself to winning, dominance, control and the shallow gratifications that were left to me. None of it would be inspired or sanctified, but would have a dull, methodical quality to it, like the stamping machine at the automobile plant, with occasional chaotic and rageful outbursts. I knew in my blood, as I believe we all still do, as I did as a boy fishing driftwood elders from the River Raisin, that life was meant to be more than this, and I was profoundly angry that the meaning I craved was being kept from me. That's how my body held it—that what I needed was being denied me and someone, by god, would pay for the injustice.

Now that I am a father and experiencing that initiation, I often wonder what would happen to a child who was listened to, set free to express his own natural passions and encouraged to be his authentic self. Would this child, growing up in the rich soil of his value and importance, flower naturally into a man of purpose and vision? Would he become responsible and generative of a healthy community and walk a path more beautiful than destructive?

I am reminded of a story Buckminster Fuller shared at a gathering of 600 in an auditorium where I sat in 1974. He told of being a boy and asking the adults around him what were the bright lights in the sky at night. He was told—again in innocence—not to be concerned with wondering about such things. His elders told him to go and play like the other boys and wait until he grew up to look at the sky. And so again, a boy's passion was shut down, his spirit of wonder put on hold. Fuller told us he felt helpless for years into his adult life, as if there was no place for him to fit in.

At the age of thirty, he found himself on the shores of Lake Michigan ready to walk into the choppy water and take his life. Even at that age and as brilliant as he was despite his difficulties, he still felt lost, unable to find his place, and felt it might be better to die. How many of us, in our own way, know this story too? Growing up lost, so stifled and trained out of our natural instincts to live a full life, wishing to end the pain, considering suicide? Just last week a young man of twenty-one here in the community drove his Ford Explorer into the woods, hooked a hose up from his exhaust pipe to the cab and killed himself. I hear of these stories all too often, and still personally struggle at times with the profound despair these young men feel. When Buckminster Fuller stood at the threshold of his despair on the shore of Lake Michigan, convinced that his attempt to compress himself into the mold that was required of him could no longer be maintained, he remembered the passions he had felt as a boy. He remembered his own children and their beauty and wanted to be a part of nurturing that spirit. And he made a decision to follow his passions regardless of the cultural pressures to do otherwise. He would live a full life, look at the stars in the night sky and wonder, and live in that wonder. Many of us know the impact Fuller had in the world, blessing millions and encouraging them to open their hearts.

Most of us aren't Buckminster Fuller, or Joseph Campbell, or Robert Bly, and we find ourselves waist deep in the icy water, unable to go forward and complete the act, and unable to retreat to shore and seek another way. We stand there half frozen, our genitals withered and withdrawn, staring into the bleakness of a gray horizon, and somehow survive. Bitterness and envy become the heat that keeps us from freezing; a low deep resentment burns. It is a slow and excruciating death, a stubborn, spiteful, silent protest. Somewhere still we know our birthright, and we keep our icy vigil in honor of it. I can't fully express the sadness of this image. It's all too real, not metaphor but truth, a futility I feel in my body and at times feel crushed by, knowing the extent to which the men in our culture suffer. What makes it worse is the prevailing attitude that presumes men have it made, that they feel no pain and are content in their Lazy Boy recliners and their 12-packs of Bud watching sports all weekend. In truth, both women and men are responsible for the world as it exists, and share equally in the loss of meaning. To me this portrayal of modern men is another form of prejudice that tries to find blame by separation. Many of us suffer from the absence of meaning, our lost passions and the poignancy of a longing unfulfilled.

What we suffer from, it seems in many cases, is a disembodied existence. The technologies we rely on, automobiles, televisions, computers, do so much of the work for us, our bodies and the body wisdom that comes through the blood of ages atrophies, and we seem to float outside of ourselves. We are unable to connect with the meaning available to us, because we are not connected to ourselves and the receptors that can receive the meaning. My call to men, often in the work of reconnecting to meaning, is to find a body sense of it, to find the weight in the flesh and bones, the structure of the soul temple that carries us through the world. It is no less than this: a soul temple that houses and is itself inseparable from our being. From this place of dropping down in—so many great teachers have spoken of this need to go down and in instead of up and away—we come to questions of weight and gravity. Only from the inner body can we come to the essential question: upon what do we stand? In the weight and substance of our mass, the literal and simple force of our structure pressing down on the earth, we can experience the degree to which meaning supports us. This is a frightening descent in many ways. The very reason, possibly, our culture is so attracted to outer space and the freedoms and infinite possibilities it appears to present, is that we are afraid to find out what it is we truly stand upon, what it is we truly represent, and that our dropping down would become a free fall into a terrible nothingness. I believe that without this dropping down, into whatever is there or isn't there for us, we will never know where we stand, never be able to make a stand or be about anything of chosen value. Prayer has been for many a sort of parachute for this descent, a comfort and mirror so that we don't lose ourselves.

Luisah Teish,[16] a story teller in the West African Yoruba traditions, speaks of how the children are taught to grow strong shoulders in their spiritual lives. They are taught this while they are also shown how their meaning depends on the strong shoulders their ancestors grew and upon which they now stand. So in this tradition there is a combination of gratitude and responsibility, a feeling of having a place to drop into with full weight and the knowledge that the future ancestors will depend on them to have a place to put their weight. Thus, the connection to meaning for all people is continued.

If we lose one child to addiction, to suicide or a half life based on consumerism alone, we lose shared beauty that is more than a concept but truly the habitat of our souls. And so my plea to men and women is to find out what holds you to the earth, then to plow and mine these strata and set deep pylons and pour your own blood and passion as if into the forms of concrete foundations, for yourselves, yes, but also and equally, for the children. This is the effort that can lead to trust, of ourselves and the wealth of our own potential continually being born. How many of us can say that we truly love, respect and bless every inch of ourselves, every ounce of body and being we lay upon the earth? If not, then what is it we offer our children to stand upon? What sort of fractured, broken, dangerous floor do we make available? Or do we make it available at all? Do we even step up at all or acknowledge at all the responsibility we have to our lineage? These are the questions that inspire me. I wonder, often, perhaps too often, out loud and to the chagrin of my family and friends, how do we turn the mistakes of our immaturity, the falseness and aggressiveness of our arrogance, into the soul compost we can draw on for our own betterment, our groundedness? I can't sit around stewing anymore about what was done to me, or how I screwed up, and bemoan the losses I have suffered. No! The losses have been my greatest teachers. The losses, the foolishness, the wise elders I have spurned, the frivolous hedonistic folly, the sex and drugs and false gypsy wandering, these are the products of my habitat, the holdings of my compost pile, and by god I'd better work with them or I'll find myself free falling and there will be nothing there to catch me.

It is perhaps a truism to state that we humans are an evolving species, in concert with all of nature and the very planet and universe around us. What may not be as apparent is that we are evolving spiritually as well as physically and that there is no difference between the two. Some would say, and I too have felt this way at times, that we have lost the ancient ways, that humans are actually devolving spiritually as time goes by. I now believe this cannot be true. How could we possibly go backwards to some golden age, some civilization that appears to have achieved the highest in spiritual evolution? What hope is there for us in this perspective? And so I state here, and work in support of the vision that we are evolving, and it is imperative to put attention and energy toward it every day, every moment even, whenever we are able. We believe that we are building on the ways of our ancestors and creating a brighter future. It is tempting to bemoan the crass consumerism of our age, the life energy robbed by televisions and computers and cellular phones. I am not convinced this moves us forward in any way. The medical intuitive Carolyn Myss[17] says that we attract to ourselves the difficulties and suffering we experience through the way we hold such things; that the only way to healing is through love, not hatred. Martin Luther King, Jr., said: "Darkness cannot drive out darkness. Only life can do that. Hate cannot drive out hate. Only love can do that." And so in respect to this wisdom, I submit that we are evolving—most likely very, very slowly. The musician and composer Lori Anderson was talking with the avant-garde composer John Cage and asked him if things are getting better or worse. He said he thought they were getting better, but at such a pace one could hardly comprehend the improvement. This appeals to me, and in my experience working with people, it matches what seems to be true of the soul; it operates at a pace much slower than the mind. The soul seems to need more time with things and works in a non-linear fashion. And so it follows that the language of the soul, or the mode of working, is ritual, and ritual is the vehicle through which our collective spiritual evolution can travel. Ritual becomes belief, belief becomes meaning, meaning then becomes the present truth. Ritual then is the tool, or the active element, in meaning.

As we know through the long history of human society, ritual can either create or destroy life. It has not always been a tool for evolution, but has been captured as a powerful animal and harnessed to the collective need in people for ritual—and their natural attraction to it—for the purposes of destruction. We need only look at the ways masterful tyrants have enlisted ritual on behalf of their megalomaniacal visions to help them accomplish their aims. Later on, there will be a more in-depth explanation of the responsibilities required to use ritual as a tool for positive evolution. Suffice to say for now, in the context of meaning, that ritual serves, and it serves me personally, as it has many if not all of my mentors, through prayer.

Prayer and the small personal rituals I have developed out of my longing and desire for meaning provide bookends to my day. In my own way, I am connected to the ancient practice, described earlier in the story of the Mohican man, and available to us in the stories of countless humans, aboriginal or modern, who invite and invoke the mystery into their lives with prayer. To greet the sun with an openness to guidance and service of Spirit, and to close with thanks, letting go, dumping of the days events in the compost heap of the dream time, and pray that another rebirth will occur in the morning, that the sun will rise again and I will get another chance, all of this and more becomes for me the structure upon which I stand and allows me to continue with my commitment to the soul life of the people. I can barely do it, even with the most profound assistance.

In my work with men, I encounter the same yearnings I experience within myself. I see it in the faces of the young men and women who attend rites of passage programs. Through our council sessions, our dancing and music, our tears and laughter, it becomes clear that all of us yearn for and are replenished by meaningful ritual. This is apparent in the many commonplace rituals of wedding, funeral, baptism, bar- and bat-mitzvah, graduation, anniversary. These ritualized events—

and many countless others—provide the lubrication that keeps our lives from freezing in place. I'm not sure if we truly appreciate their significance, but they certainly are vital and sustaining.

I have said before that there is little gain to be made in bemoaning our culture and the loss of meaning we have experienced in the modern time. I can recall walking down the outdoor mall in Boulder with elder and healer Eric Leonardson, beginning to engage in carping about the commercialism pressing in on us from all sides. He said, "This is the way you want it." That's a hard one to grasp, but becomes more and more relevant to me as I take back my projections and learn what Jung talked about when he said, "As is within, so is without." So this is our world, and if there is any hope of change, we must embrace it. In this spirit, I believe it is helpful to the process to name some of what I see. I have sat with too many men who devoted their lives to the accepted belief that a nice house and car and an impressive stock portfolio and an executive position would feed their desire for meaning. Undoubtedly for some, it does work. But for so many, there is an emptiness, an absence of passion, of love and caring and a deep sense of purpose. Those who are happy basking in the cultural paradigm of the American dream have their place. There is ample space for their dreams to unfold. But what of those who aren't inspired by the dream? What of those who find its structure unstable, even dangerous and destructive to life? Do we carve out a space for these people? Is their vision honored? It appears to me not nearly enough, and for that reason I write. I'm not interested in some sort of new age inquisition against corporate America and the machinery of capitalism. All I'm saying is that many of us, and more and more of us, are finding the expression of meaning we currently live in unfulfilling. What may be helpful would be to look at the relationship that corporate America has to the environment, the people, and the earth as a living body. In this way we may find the messages and clues that will guide us to a more promising future. There are many alternatives that I pray we continue to explore.

As I CONSIDER THE WAYS MEANING HAS TOUCHED ME IN MY work and life, it has had a quality similar to a veil falling away. That which separated me or blocked me from my passion gave way to lucidity. I respect the many ways this happens to us, and yet for me there is an energy, a force that is tangible in the body, a vibration, a rush, a different way of seeing, and the separation I feel from myself and nature falls away. I am able at these times to hold and take in a true flavor for human nature and in particular to appreciate the wisdom of the elders. In doing so, my ancestors' lives are acknowledged, and an opening to their support is created. These awarenesses sustain me through my days and nights.

In times of transition, I have noticed we often come to our lives without a ground of meaning, the energy or support necessary to make the passage. The elders aren't there—or we don't know about them—and the ancestors are suspect at best. Each trip around the sun sends us irrevocably into the new seasons of our lives, yet we may be, in some peculiar way, along only for the ride. We may find ourselves behind a veil, lost in a confusion, a sort of energy density that holds us with fear, resistance, harsh judgments, old wounds and unresolved conflicts. It seems that so often the passages in our society are blurred, they go unacknowledged, and we let them go by, or they pass in an awkward, clumsy way. Their gifts are lost to us, and we fail to grow and evolve as people. The ancient cultures knew how essential these gateways were, and the mythologies of world peoples are filled with stories of these passages, what they mean, why we must go through them as consciously as possible.

I am reminded of an adolescent boy who accompanied us into the boundary waters of northern Minnesota. We encouraged him to spend the night alone on an island. We told him we would pray for him all night, and so he had the support of three men, a backbone for the journey. I will never forget watching him stroke his paddle through the water, his back to us, his gear loaded in the canoe, and us on the shore,

chanting, one of us with a drum, another with a rattle. This was not some prescribed method. It happened spontaneously, as was wanted and needed with the veil between us fallen. At one point he looked back at us, and he did not smile. He was in the gateway, launching himself into the next phase of his life. As soon as he hit shore on the island, we stopped our music. He had crossed. The water itself was his threshold.

Once he landed, he knew he couldn't come back. Those watching were equally touched, and knew we were called to be there at these times. We stood around the fire and cried, realizing how important it is for men to be there for the boys, and we too engaged a passage into a sense of purpose, a calling that goes deep in our bones to show up for these critical times of transition. The image of that boy, and the wisdom that came to his support team around the fire, continue to enrich and teach me, even after twelve years. This is the power of such things. The beginning, middle and end overlap with what has been and what will be.

We were standing on the shore of a wilderness lake, we had bushwhacked through swamp and had come through great physical difficulty to find this lake filled with giant snapping turtles and big walleye and eagles circling, the smell of decay in the forest. At one point we caught a couple of fat walleye and had them resting on the shore while we set up camp. I heard a noise down by the shore and went to investigate. A giant snapping turtle, its sharp-bumped shell dark green and brown

streaked with moss growing on it, had eaten half of a fish and was drag-
ging the other by the tail into the lake. We were counting on those fish
for dinner, but here we were in the wilderness and the rules were not
ours to make. We were wrapped in this example of death and rebirth,
the nature of the forest, and the continual renewal and passage through
the thresholds, the death of our old ways, our smaller selves. If we're
unable to notice our passages, the old ways cling to us, and leave us less
able to grow into the next season, to face the next challenge or be present for the next call to help another in transition. Nature itself, while we
were in its womb, held us in this way. It understood the necessity of our
birth, and the beginning of our own life of transitions. The death of our
life's previous stage is necessary for the next opportunity of life to
emerge. I met with this boy nine years later, and we talked of that time
he went out alone. He was filled with warmth and pride at the memory, and still stands on that foundation and draws on it for meaning and
purpose. He finds strength in his well honored and witnessed crossing
into manhood.

He wrote a letter about that night, recalling how he had prayed next
to a fire and was moved to carve a mask representing his childhood. He
worked at the birch bark alone on the island. A nearby tree suddenly
fell, loud and frightening in the giving up of its hold on the earth. It
startled him, but he soon returned to carving out the days of boyhood,
the wounds and wonderment, knowing he would leave it there and die
to his boyhood in the dying light of a lonely fire. "When I awoke, I was
a man," he wrote. Blessed be.

As I celebrate this boy's passage, so too I mourn the countless youth
who have no island to paddle to, who will not know the ancestral linkage that occurred for that boy and us men, whose blood will be cut off
from that strong replenishing source and will have to go it alone. I imagine the unheard longing of our souls crying out from veiled places, dis-
connected, disembodied, in between and lost, like fruit hit by frost
before it ripens, hard and green, their full sweetness never to be tasted.
I hold this image with profound sadness, and I long and pray that it can
be different. I can't help but see our current times—as wonderful as they
are in many ways—as times of grief, and in the grief, through the grief,

the way is opened once again, the threshold becomes manifest out of the fog, and we are invited to pass.

It seems to me Spirit continually invites us back, and we as humans have the unique capacity of choice, the ability to inquire, to ponder, to wonder and observe. If we can slow down long enough to go into ourselves, it often becomes clear to us in a thousand ways that our passages require attention. They ask to be honored and engaged in fully for the continued evolution of ourselves and our people. I have no doubt the information is available to us all, in the strong winds, sheets of rain, warming sun and the spreading petals of a wild daisy—the vision of a life that is to be lived and must be lived in all of its beauty and horror. This call will come to us so long as people roam the earth.

For those who hear the voice and are wondering how to act on it, behold the elders. These are the men and women who have made the passage into old age, who have carried forth the ancestral blood, who encountered the support of their own elders and take responsibility now for the soul of their communities. These elders provide a blessing force for their people, through their endurance and faith, their accumulated experience and the cultivation of their authentic natures. As I have witnessed elders alive and free in their truth and awareness of what really matters, I have an unmistakable knowing of their incredible importance to the rest of us making healthy passages into maturity.

When I am in the presence of an elder, a heat floods my body. I feel it as a soul food, a mysterious royal jelly (the most nutritious food a beehive produces, given only to the larvae that will grow into queens). The elders exude this quality of grace that feeds our souls and can sustain us through the difficult passages into our own sovereignty. Without elders the dangerous power of unrefined ferocity can break out and destroy beauty. I am reminded of the final First Nation people to be subjugated. The story goes that a band of warriors was still at large, even though all of the chiefs and elders had surrendered. Without the direction, guidance and restraint of the elders, this band of warriors marauded the countryside, killing everything in their path they saw as the enemy. No doubt their frustration and futility had its foundation in the loss of their land and way of life. Be that as it may, the elders were able to recognize the time to lay down arms and accept defeat with honor. The youth untouched by their stable wisdom lost all honor and became in some ways worse than their oppressors. Without that royal jelly of the elders feeding their souls, the warriors could not act like tribal chiefs. I don't think any of us could have. How many youth today are in this same condition?

It worries me that elders in our time are so often separated from the rest of us. An elder outside of the community cannot flower his or her potential into the world. If you've spent much time in nursing homes, it's easy to see the truth of this in the faces of those wise ones with no one to counsel. All of us suffer when we are unable to sit with the compassion and fierce loyalty to heart matters and surrender to worldly concerns the elders often embody. And we are left unprepared to make our passage into elderhood when the community calls on us to do so. I feel this as a gap in the teeth that the tongue continually returns to, surprised nothing is there, looking again and again for that which naturally belongs in the space. The longing is so strong in me and the men I work with, we've taken to the practice of admiring old men whenever we see them. Just watching and appreciating the stiffness of the walk or the lines of age, the baldness or raspiness of voice, feeds a little bit of that longing. And of course, whenever possible, the opportunity to sit with elders must be taken, even if on the surface they appear to be not so wise. I advocate a receptivity to such relationships—on the part of both the young ones and the elders—to give and receive the nurturing of the heart, the connection to ancestral meaning and the biological wisdom of how humans thrive and evolve.

Who chooses us or whom we choose as elder, whether living or dead, human or not, is important and best not be taken lightly. For it is true that many elders have not been able, for various reasons of disenchantment, to take on the mantle of heart and generative presence in that season of their lives. In the prayer of being open to finding one's elder and spiritual team, let the body be your reference point of truth. The body, like a tuning fork, will tell you when the resonance is right between you and another. For some, it will come as "uh-huh, yes;" for others it may be a warmth in the chest. Another may hear a certain sound. We all have our ways of noticing the body's wisdom that are natural to us. This in itself is an act of prayerful being.

One time I was in the Berkshire Mountains of Western Massachusetts helping guide a men's retreat to explore meaning and prayer. It was one of our bi-annual gatherings to inquire together and express our life stories in a respectful circle. I've always made it a point at any of these gatherings around the country to observe the energy and attempt to read the authenticity of spirit and soul present. I take it as my responsibility to track the depth and watch the movement of each group's healing vision and manifestation of meaning through the questions, dialogue, creative expression, prayers and meditations that occur. What I have observed is that the quest for meaning, the yearning to understand individual purpose and inspiration, is difficult to sustain without elders at the gathering. It's not so much that the elders speak profoundly or offer some great teaching that bowls people over. It's more in the physical presence, a quality of connection to history, lineage, blood, that produces a vital charge—very tangible—of encouragement. All of us benefit, even the other elders, and find the strength to step through whatever passage lies before us. It seems that the elder, standing at the brink of that most mysterious and daunting of passages, has let go of the more cultural, material and selfish dilemmas that consume younger men. The elder knows a deep faith and has developed an intimacy with the greater and everlasting truths of life.

At this one gathering in the Berkshires, thirty or forty of us had formed a community that we all knew would last only three days, but had been here forever and would last equally as long. I want to digress here for a moment and comment on how quickly and naturally humans form generative communities when the elements are there for such flowering. All over the country, up in Canada, wherever I have gone, the community pops up, fully formed after just a few hours together. I am always filled with hope at these gatherings. I am certain when I am there that whatever problems face us, there is within us a natural ability to resolve them and bring us closer together. All we need to do—and I know this is much more difficult than I'm expressing—is find the combination of ingredients to let our shared vision emerge. I know it will emerge if given the chance.

So here we were, wondering together about the sources of meaning and fullness in our lives. What blocks us from our sense of love for self and other? we asked each other. We had created a container to hold such questions and allow us the safety to be ourselves. Each of us brought a unique story, a means of accessing the inspiration that sustains us. Together, we had the potential to deepen our soul waters, to find the aqueducts to our ancestors and the allies in nature and our spirit lives that could help us. The tension and anticipation electrified our bodies. The presence of ancestors in the collective field around us, in our own blood, was very tangible. We could feel it in the wind that touched our faces and smell it rise up from the loamy earth upon which we sat. There was this quality of truth, an energetic substance, that felt like returning home after a lengthy absence, a sudden restoration of respect, for self and place. The tension continued to build and appeared in no hurry to leave. It would, in fact, provide the basis for our entire time together, a sort of energy matrix out of which would come our charge, and onto which we could project and observe our own ways of being. I can't tell you how electrifying and dangerous these times are at the beginning of gatherings like this. No one knows what will happen and yet everyone waits for it and expects it. What was it to be?

As if by mistake or accident, the next ingredient presented itself: it was to welcome and thank the elders for coming, for enduring life and maintaining heart. The elder men came forward, and we acknowledged them, and their ancestors who had come before and made it possible for these men to be with us now. These elders came forward slowly, with apprehension and uncertainty. Perhaps they expected to be blamed for what had gone wrong, criticized for perpetuating a destructive patriarchy. I can't say for sure, but it was clear they didn't know what to expect and came forward in doubt. One of these men, Bob Coté, came to me later and spoke. He told me that many elders, himself included, had never been acknowledged, never been seriously brought into the passage with respect and spirit, into their own power as elders. And so I could feel once again how vital the process of marking, "the welcoming" and passage is to humans, both women and men, throughout our lives.

If there are no ripe elders there to welcome middle-aged and young adult men and women into the next stage, a type of vacuum occurs that holds them in between, neither old nor young. The unwelcomed stand upright in this vacuum as if held there like targets on a shooting range. It is no surprise that so many people, teenagers, middle-aged, the old, are shot down in these transition times, when no one is there to pull them through the vacuum. We lose them to alcohol and drugs, suicide and disease.

At this one gathering, when the elders took their place of honor in front of us and were asked to share in the guidance of our time together, the dangerous and electric charge that pulled us upward dropped in an instant. I could feel the room come into itself and the men drop into their bodies, as if some great being had come among us from the surrounding forest and drove a stake into the ground at our feet and declared, "You are here! You are a holy man. You belong and so do I." Shortly after, we walked back over the rocky terrain to our bunks. We were ready for the dream time and could sleep in peace, some of us anyway, because the village had its rightful order. The elders had claimed the position of respect, and the rest of us could settle into where we belonged from there.

Sometimes this is when the coyotes come out of the hollows. During one of our week-long gatherings the tradition was to do a ceremonial sweat purification prayer (a pan-cultural tradition) during the middle of the week, as a death and rebirth ritual. I had been pouring sweats for seven years, after having built fires and hauled water for my elders who taught me the sweat prayer way. It had become part of our tradition for me to help the men build the sweat fire in a prayerful way. Another ritual, sort of a shadow to the main ritual, was that one of my elders—who has become a working partner—would come to the fire pit just before lighting and begin to dismantle the wood and rock structure we had spent hours on, telling us we had done it all wrong and it would never burn. As the years passed, and this secondary tradition continued, I began to find great humor in the moment of embarrassment when all of these men who had falsely been looking to me for guidance, saw me lose face in the presence of the elder. During the first few years of this,

I didn't see the humor, but over time I began to appreciate the value of being a fool, when the fool has been revealed to everyone. Allowing myself to play the part, I realized a certain authenticity came into the ritual. The fool showing up belies the idea that control and precision can make it right—somehow above reproach. In truth, the elder was always right. There *was* less of a chance of the fire going well. This particular elder and I continue to work together and deepen in respect for our different ways.

We can look to the cultures of the world for examples of how this works. A First Nation people, the Cherokee, call it "the understanding." It is the path into communion with the elders and the ancestors, to the way of knowing and the utility of it. For the Cherokee—as best as I can know it—this quest for understanding is the purpose of life. This desire to gain proximity to the wisdom of the generations motivates and inspires a quiet dedication. We can see it manifest in the ways of so many people from such diverse places. All of us share the biology and spirit that compels us to such awareness. I believe we want to go there, because it is the place most conducive to thriving and the flowering of our beauty. The elders teach us this.

In our current cultural milieu, much attention is given to the lost youth, the violent teenage boys, the unwed young mothers…and on and on. These conditions occupy our attention, and we seek solutions directly in them, imagining we must do something to our adolescents to fix whatever is wrong with them. My experience leads to a different solution. It lies with the elders. The problems of our youth are a mirror of our neglected elders.

So often I have encountered people who have reached the age of elderhood, but are not there in spirit. They have come to a worn down state physically and spiritually, and have not been well lubricated with soul grease and find their bones catching on one another. Weariness and defeat holds many of them in a captive state. Out of touch with meaning and purpose, unappreciated by their communities (and often their own families), they descend into a kind of half life. In a weakened state, they accept a culture that doesn't serve them or their people. Without them vital and alive and questioning the present values, youth are lost,

and will remain lost until honorable transitions into maturity are celebrated, marked and integrated into daily life.

The experience of elders who have not been cut off rekindles the
knowledge of their importance to the proper order of things. I feel the
desire for this in my body as a longing, a real pain that can only be
soothed by sitting with an elder. Something about being in the dynamic of one who has survived a long and difficult life quenches a thirst in
me. I can recall the time Sir Laurens van der Post came through Boulder
in one of his last public appearances before he died. He was in his 80's
and had to be helped onto the stage. Even then he needed the assistance
of a cane in each hand to help him walk, bent over and unsteady. At one
point he stopped, pulled himself erect, held his arms up in the air with
the canes and shook them at the sky. The people cheered and cried and
were transported by the power and dignity of this man who had dedicated his life to spirit and meaning. He had taken our appreciation of
him, done some internal expansion of it, and poured it back on us ten-
fold. The feeling in that room brought such blessed grace to all of us,
and was generated by the essence of elderhood. The reassurance I felt in
those days with Sir Laurens brought me healing and inspriation, that
even in these times of such stimulation and confusion that soul inspiration literally has to fight for survival, there are still paragons of evolved
humanity who walk with dignity into the twilight years of their final
passage.

If I could shatter one myth, one cultural presumption, it would be
the idea that a life dedicated to material success and hierarchical climbing will culminate in happiness and salvation. The elders I have worked
with who bought into this myth, who gave their souls to it, who missed
the growing up of their children for it, who gave up their dreams and
inspirations in homage to it, have said (almost to a man) it means little
if anything to them now. They express more often a sense of betrayal, a
feeling of being sold a lie that has left them drained of inspiration and
joy. In their souls, after all is said and done, the retirement package is in
order, the life insurance policies current, the summer home paid off, the
original soul yearning comes back and pounds on their chest bones—
sometimes it's literally cardiac arrest—and says, "What about me!" It's

not just that the men have gotten lost individually. There's the added force of a collective disappointment, a society that knows something is missing and is collapsing in its absence.

Just for a moment, I would like to depart and speak about money. Those that know me know also that I struggle with my own shadows about money. I have come to a surprising conclusion—one that continues to evolve. Money is sacred. It is as sacred as anything. Our problems with it are linked to the profane label placed on it. If money is the root of all evil, and a rich man can't get into heaven, then it follows that the American pursuit of happiness based on getting ahead will inevitably become sick and twisted. Deep down, there is guilt and confusion about making and spending money. In many ways, it is the shadow relationship with money that makes us so bewitched and manipulated by it. If people valued money as a sacred expression of the soul's desires, a means by which to act responsibly in the world, I believe there would be less waste, less excess and greed and judgments of superiority based on wealth. This is a subject that fascinates me (betwixt and between, what voices are burning to be heard?).

Although the temptation is strong to bemoan our situation and sit helplessly pining for the elders who aren't there, for the community that will embrace us, the teachers that will usher us through our passages, I do not advocate it. A certain amount of seeing things for what they are will help us move out of victimhood and into self-direction. A young man at a recent gathering of wilderness guides advised us to stop imagining there is community available for the youth of today. It isn't there, and what he asked us to do is stop idealizing and teach young people the skills to develop their own spiritual lives. The ability to cultivate an elder presence within ourselves, through study, and calling into our lives the memory of proud and wise maturity, can help fill the void. So many men I know are still waiting for their fathers to love them. The rub here is that fathers for all time have often been unable to love their sons as they wanted to be loved, and yet men can discover that their fathers did love them, in ways that weren't always easy to see or take in. Some of the men still waiting on *ideal* father love are elders themselves and yet they are caught in that no man's land of incomplete transition. It's much harder alone, and it would be better, most of the time, had our fathers and grandfathers been there for their sons. When you're sitting in an apple orchard, it's wise to develop a taste for apples. Perhaps some of what is presented here can help to whet the palate.

Several years ago I was in New Jersey at a YMCA camp with a group of men. Once again, we called the elders forward, acknowledged them and asked them to be as much an active part of the gathering as felt right to them. For all the reasons previously stated, I knew this would engage all of us on a deeper level. Shortly after the elders stepped out to be seen, a very bright and engaging young man stepped forth to challenge the elders. He wondered why he should trust them. He told us that none of us had any context in his life; we were strangers and he didn't feel safe automatically trusting someone because of age. His point served us all, and in some ways demonstrated the magic of elder energy. He stepped out and was seen, because the elders were out there to see him. If we hadn't called them forward, there would have been nowhere for him to go with his mistrust. He wouldn't have been able to help us see a cultural attitude of suspicion. We have so thoroughly convinced ourselves that the older generation has nothing to offer, that their ways are why things are so messed up, that we cannot experience the mirroring of our own purpose and value that is possible through strong elder contact. And the truth, as I have seen it, is that many elders have become bitter, wracked with the pain of isolation.

I recall the first time I encountered Steven Foster and Meredith Little,[18] who have conducted solo fasting rites of passage and vision training near Death Valley for thirty years. I came back from my four days alone, and they spent three-and-a-half hours listening to and mirroring back my story. I had never experienced such a realm and felt like I must be on another planet. The patience and attention and concentration required to hold me so completely, with such love and respect, truly seemed superhuman, on the one hand, and completely natural and normal on the other. All the while, Steven chipped at a piece of glass that he shaped into an arrowhead and gave to me when he and Meredith were finished hearing me. Every facet in that glass held another reflection of the experience I had in the desert, and helped me to remember and integrate it, through the attention given to the carvers art, and through the even more profound art of listening. This perhaps more than anything else is the value of refined elderhood. One who has come through all the striving, who has seen the folly of his judgments, the absurdity of his opinions, can be a crystal clear and calm pool in which younger souls can see themselves.

Yes, there are elders who want to dictate what we do, who criticize and tell us we're doing it wrong. Sometimes this may be exactly what is needed. If it isn't needed, the community is responsible to make that known. It is the community that ultimately makes the elder, calls the man or woman into the role. If a person of elder age doesn't enhance the life of the people, then it is right and good for the community to refuse that person elder status. An elder of mine spoke of the old way of becoming an elder based on the accumulated acts of a lifetime. Elder status is given because the individual has shown responsibility and dedication, and can be trusted to care for the spirit of the people. The great religions have carried out this practice from the beginning.

In our current situation, so few elders function vitally, and it is difficult for those coming into their fifties and sixties to know how it is they can best serve and be served. The map has been lost and the elders, wandering, looking for home, are swept up and housed together in places separate from the community. This is perhaps our greatest American tragedy.

One time many years ago I was invited to a gathering of First Nation Native American men for a healing encampment in South Park, Colorado. The First Nation elders from tribes across America called the council because they believed (through a series of synchronous dreams) the men and people needed it, and the earth was in trouble, also. I was honored with an invitation out of my respect for the old ways. I can remember turning off of Highway 285 and heading north on a dirt road flanked by the Collegiate Range, part of our country's backbone, the Continental Divide. Snow had already begun to accumulate on the 14,000 foot peaks, though it was still summer. The dirt road snaked through the hilly, treeless country, carved by little drainages dotted with willow and chokecherry bushes. The sky was such a deep blue you could almost leap up and dive into it and swim in an ocean of eternity and endless mystery defined by islands of lacy cumulus clouds. Up ahead, it seemed as if the clouds had fallen and landed on a plateau. As I drove closer, I could see there were clusters of teepees circling a large meadow. I drove into this encampment with some apprehension, being among the few white people invited.

Much of what happened there was private and I cannot speak of it. Elders came forward from all over North America to this gathering of somewhere around a thousand men. At one point a Lakota elder, grizzled and leathery, etched by the harsh seasons and a lifetime of honorable defeat, took the stage and spoke to the young men. "Yes, it is true," he said, "the white man came to our homeland and took everything from us, our land, our food, our dignity, our way of life—almost everything. What he didn't take was our heart and soul. You must never stop dancing. Even if there is only one of you left, keep dancing. That can *never* be taken from you."

His words seemed to come straight through him from the ancestors. A truth thousands of years old silenced the crowd. What he said without directly saying it, was about the danger of giving up. People knew what he meant, that to give up that last bastion of spirit was in essence a death wish, not just for us as individuals, but for all of the people. He spoke very slowly and the silence between his words filled with a wind that carried the ancient meaning. No one could stand up and debate him. I believe all of us knew how correct he was, and with what we were being charged. I will never forget him.

Not only had he spoken a timeless truth about the ways of spirit, he had claimed the ground reserved for elders. A young man saying the same thing would almost certainly have come across arrogant or aggressive or presumptuous. The words had to come out of an old wrinkled body, on the wings of a voice scratched and battered with experience, a voice that had lamented and cursed into endless winter nights and not been heard. That voice could give us hope. That voice could cut through our opinions and help us see how important it is to keep dancing and praying and never surrender to the modern gods of greed, dominance and indifference to others. That voice could deliver the gravity of our responsibility into our a knapsacks, and would not feel heavy or burdensome, but could be carried forward as a blessing from the ancestors.

The elder can be heard because he or she knows the wisdom of a poem by Pablo Naruda, *The Well*, that says, "Shake off my word that came to wound you and let it fly through the open window. It will return to wound me without your guiding it," and in this way becomes a teaching. Mature elders have reached the time of letting go, and from that freedom can see more clearly the larger forces at play in life. They have given up their "cherished outcomes," to quote a Druid vow of friendship, and have an openness to diversity. Another elder, a local man Ted Warren, said not long ago, "Why should I ever force my judgments and opinions on others?" His question struck me, not only because of its humility, but the subtle message. The key word is "force." The forcing of things results in clearcutting forests or a religious principle that implies the lives of those who believe otherwise have less value. It's the diversity of the different voices that brings forth the strength of a system. To force is to dominate and is out of sync with the way of forest and tundra. In these healthy systems, each species struggling for survival creates niches and nooks for the other species. There is a movement to dominate, to have dominion over others for species survival, but to be in a relentless program of domination is to eventually defeat oneself. The species that finds itself alone, that has choked out all competition, all opposing ways, will surely choke itself out also, as a matter of course.

Elders, the ones not so broken, are the ones among us who know this, who have refined the art of tolerance through countless defeats and failures, and even more relevant, from the victories that hurt others and in the end proved meaningless. When an elder like Ted Warren, who lives here in our small community, speaks about not forcing judgments and opinions on others, his words have weight. He knows from experience, from, I presume, having at times forced his way and witnessed the outcome. Does that mean young people should be prevented from holding righteous views and ideals they might force on others? No. It does mean, however, that in the absence of distinguished elders who are revered, young people have no barometer of their impact on the community, no gauge and no limits. Without checks and balances, youthful indignation can quickly degenerate into senseless violence, like it did, as the tale goes, with the First Nation warriors who fought on after their leaders had surrendered, as it does for many youth today, who haven't got authentic guiding forces, and whose frustrations often turn to violence.

Robert Bly once told me it is important to have strong opinions. It is like the rose, he said, with a strong aroma that spreads out and touches all life in the meadow. Strong opinions are a sign of passion, a way of spreading beauty in the striving and competition of our audacious existence. I have learned to value the strength of opinions expressed in my various circles. My radar goes off, though, when an opinion is clenched in a tight fist that has no room for air, light or contradictions. My neck hairs bristle when someone's opinion represents a position of superiority that wants to control and overpower others. I do not imagine the wild rose stands in the tundra and says to the other plants, "You must smell like me to be in God's grace." No! Its strong fragrance is an invitation, a call to bees, butterflies, moths, beetles and other roses informing them it is in bloom and ready to dance. The kind of opinions I believe Mr. Bly spoke of are similar. They are opinions that bloom, that speak of the yearning, open the inquiry and invite the vigorous and loving debates. These dilemmas found in the human experience, further the choice of available destinies of kindness, compassion and healing.

The elders I have known speak with the wisdom of the tundra. They, like wild roses, know their survival depends on the countless ways different from their own. And so the elders advocate more religions, not less. They speak of evolving new and personal forms of spirituality. They suggest re-evaluation of traditional systems we may have abandoned in our youth. They advocate an open heart that can be reached with God's word in whatever form it may present itself.

Could it be our very survival cries out for attention from the elders—Great Spirit, Jesus, Goddess, whatever force, energy or condition that moves one in right relation to his destiny? Our very survival cries out for this. Those who have gone down this road before, implore us to give up the sixty and eighty hour work weeks and come home to our children. It is important that we listen to them when they say meaning and worthiness come in recognizing beauty, the wonder of uncertainty gambled on, the joy of loving companions, the practice of kindness, choices that bring the reality of peace into our families and communities. The longest enduring elder of them all, our earth, asks also that we listen and appreciate how the land and sky care for us without hesitation.

The First Nation people, the Hopi of the Southwest, have been leading lives of simplicity for thousands of years. They have a saying that goes, "The health of a people is known by the spiritual health of the children and the elders." In our country, the children are gasping for their spiritual breath. Many of them aren't making it. Over half of those who survive into their twenties do so for the most part by embracing a god of material wealth and consumerism. Over half of those who continue into their forties will most likely have been divorced at least once. The men who have children will spend an average of ten minutes a day with their sons and daughters. The rest of the time, television, video and computer games fill the void. How can machines possibly satisfy the children's yearning for human understanding, touch, appreciation? I imagine the Hopi elder looking at this and grimly shaking her head, in grief, and then doing something about it.

As for the elders, I cannot contain my grief at their isolation. It first hit me on a Thanksgiving Day twenty years ago. I drove down Laplaisance Avenue in Monroe, Michigan, on my way to grandma's. I looked into the old houses along the avenue and saw the elders, mostly women, alone. How could it be? On the one day in America when we take a momentary break from commercialism and give thanks with family and friends for the blessings in our lives, on *this* day, there is no place at the table for the old ones? I can't imagine a more grim picture.

I was fortunate as a boy and young man to have grandparents and great-grandparents who brought us together regularly to feast. I can vividly remember the old women crowded into great-grandma's kitchen, their full bodies draped in cotton dresses, some wearing embroidered aprons, sweating over pots of food filling every burner of the stove, the oven loaded with casseroles, pies, breads and meat. The smells of a well cooked feast, their warm voices chattering, the children and adults anxiously moving in the house, awaiting the delicacies soon to be served, raised in me not just an appetite for food, but a soul longing as well. I knew as a boy, in a way I could never have described, that the main feast here was of love. The love infused by my grandmothers into that feast is what sustains me to this day. Those women learned it well from their elders and passed it on to their children and grandchildren. In their humble generosity preparing a thanksgiving feast, the elders showed me what truly matters.

The way of the elders that teaches giving and receiving love, this is the soul food that sustains a culture. Look at the Kalahari Bush People and the Australian Aboriginals. These cultures have remained intact for fifty thousand years at least. How can we not look to them for guidance when they have endured for so long? Surely these ancient ways are the seeds of all great modern religions. How ironic that so much attention has been given to converting them from their heathen ways. In my study of these cultures, it has become clear to me the sustaining force has been love. The Kalahari people and the Australian natives found the untold beauty and meaning in the acts of giving and receiving love. Nothing else even comes close.

I don't expect this is any great revelation to anyone. It almost seems trite to express. There is little value in positing truisms, and yet I feel it must be said. A truly loving way is not trite. To me love is like dance or prayer. It can be practiced in countless ways. It's not so much how one loves, or dances, or prays; it is the devotion or inspiration that matters more. What is lacking is not an appreciation for love. You need only watch our popular movies and listen to our songs to know we appreciate love. What is lacking is a commitment to love. It is said our ancestors, in good times, spent up to three quarters of the day in some kind of prayer, dance, rite of passage, initiation. This is what it took for them to love their souls and sustain a depth of spirit that endures. I find it intriguing how much modern people have become cut off from the pulse of divine rhythms, via the loss of time to pray and contemplate. This struggle lives in my daily life as the seductions of work and outside involvements continually pull at me, drawing me away from quiet and solitude. Therein hangs one of the leading questions for modern man: are we losing ourselves and our connection to our own souls and the soul of earth? The studies that have been done on the leisure time of modern people suggest that we have less free time than people have ever had, and that it continues to shrink.

Elders and children know what it takes. They have the time. If the elders and children were listened to, we would know more of what our purpose is. Their reflections back to us would teach us what is required. We would gladly take on the tasks and responsibilities necessary to tend to our elders, and thus be tended to by them. I'm not suggesting we go back to another age. Primitive people undoubtedly had their problems. Had it been perfect, why would it have changed? Perhaps it is in the human code to make change even if it is perfect, simply for the adventure. In the modern world our lust for domain, excitement and entertainment threatens to destroy us. We have begun to look like a plant that has no roots, that floats in the ether, drawing its strength by feeding on itself. One can only think that the thrust of modern times keeps pulling us away from humanity's truths. It cannot last. When the tundra is overtaken by a single species, or when a culture is taken over by a money-dominated approach, there is no replenishing, no beneficial symbiosis. The one plant will destroy itself and everything else.

I believe we know this. Our blood, our evolution, our ancestry, our biology, sense this. Some moment of clarity opens to us, and we know. It could be while sitting next to a stream, or in a coffee shop, or driving to visit our grandfathers and grandmothers, perhaps sharing a fresh fire-baked ear of Wisconsin home-grown corn. These simple times can be psychic cusps, moments when epiphany and grace make us larger than we believed ourselves to be. Each of us carries millions of years of experience, sperm and egg, sperm and egg. Have you ever stood with yourself at the front of your lineage, and then turned one-hundred-and-eighty degrees and looked into the eyes of your parents, and your parents' parents, all the way back? Each of us has a wise elder within that can connect us to the deep truths. Yes, we live in difficult times. Yes, the god of limitless consumerism, ordained by us, has taken our land and our way of life and made us slaves and hypnotized us into the illusion of freedom by bombarding us with electronic imagery conductive of the new mythology. Still, even if there is only one of us left, as the Lakota elder said, keep dancing. That can *never* be taken from us.

I look around and see that many of us are still dancing. Independently and in groups a new and flexible culture is emerging. People are finding ways to reconnect to meaning, finding a rich soil into which roots can grow. Through simple acts of discipline and commitment, the embrace of a vision that comes from the heart of human experience, communities are establishing and reinvigorating traditions. The road maps are showing up that can take us to the core of our souls. They are coming from all of the various spiritual traditions, religions and philosophies. Much of what seems to work is connected to nature and the cycles of the seasons. This feels good and proper. Do we not continue to rotate around the same sun? Does one rotation not occupy the same amount of time? Does the earth not wobble on its axis in a predictable rhythm that carries us through the seasons? And so it makes sense that we celebrate the solstice and equinox, give thanks for the return of the sun, lament its disappearance. It seems misguided to me for modern people to imagine they can create a new society entirely independent of the old ways. This is why so much of the new age ideology disturbs me. It's too light and airy, and in its free floating form can become destructive, like lateral lightning that passes charges between clouds but is not grounded.

Evolution furthers the characteristics that serve. A salamander does not cut off its leg just because it can grow a new one. The laws of biology and the material world are not separate from how Spirit moves through all things. Any approach based on the separation of human spirit from the body and nature carries some essential flaw. And yet, it is not my place to say a creature does not belong on the tundra. If it grows and finds a place, so be it. My challenge is in staying close to the teachings of my elders and in bringing forward their blessings and encouragement. As much as anything, the earth is our preeminent elder.

The old ones taught me to support a culture inspired by the old ways, that seeks out the stories, myths, poems, artists and mystics, and takes their teaching as a road map. These tools have been offered as support, not as some form of dogma that requires my servitude. The elders who inspired me offered their teachings as stepping stones, not as definitive truths. They counseled me to take what works and leave the rest.

Their orientation is not to be placed on pedestals and followed like masters. They simply want my life to work, my gifts to come forth. They want to see me contribute to the volume of human experience, to add my ingredients to the stew pot of human potential. They don't want me to add the same ingredients they did, to cut the carrots in one way only and mince the onions a certain size. What sort of bland pabulum would that produce? Elders who have been through it have learned to recognize authenticity. That is what they have shown me has value. They ask of their descendants to be true to themselves, to follow their paths with dignity. They ask that we not forget the old ways.

I admit that for much of my life I resisted the guidance of elders. I remained numb to their wisdom. It is still tempting to fall asleep, to be entertained by the purchase of new toys, to look at what others have with "envy—the worst poison," as Robert Moore has said. What calls me home is the sweet nectar of my elders' love. They hold places in my body, are anchored there inside, and are a part of me that will never let me forget. Like the granite rocks painted with orange, red and yellow lichen, the elders give us stability, and you can actually get a hold of it. I can no longer fall asleep in front of television or let some god not of my choosing possess me. When I want to give up, to say forget it, I'm movin' north, there's nothing I can do, I am reminded the elders did not give up on me. I pray the elders know they saved my life.

One time while sitting in a circle of men with the elder Robert Bly, he said something that I have contemplated for years. Mr. Bly spoke about elders and their vital role in the community. He said, "Be with the elders in any capacity you can. It doesn't matter what the activity. You don't even have to speak with them. If you see an elder sitting on a park bench, go sit next to him or her. Simply being in the presence of an elder is enough to receive his blessing, receive her wisdom and get a sense of yourself, your life and what has importance and meaning for you." Even before I heard this, I remembered the power and heart of the elders, in grocery stores, bus stations, churches, everywhere. In noticing them, I feel a kind of essential blessing occur. Something comes into my body and soul and renews me. Simply being in proximity to age and experience provides a subtle inspiration that encourages me to carry on. These stolen encounters with elders I have never met reminds me of the old ones I did know, who loved me directly and completely. They feed my soul to this day, long after they have died. To these beautiful people I am forever grateful.

For those who are interested in tasting the unborn future, I ask you, from your great life adventure, to look back and remember, first in your mind, then melting through your body, who touched you as an elder? Human and non-human? See if there still lives a spark of energy, some numinous truth. If you are inclined, lean down, touch the earth and blow onto that spark, your life breath. Watch the many flames of elder presence rekindle and connect again. Please remember that elders come to us in infinite ways, and are already there in many shapes and sizes, waiting to grow with us into our own elderhood. I have met men who know their elders as old gnarled trees, faces on rock outcroppings, the great Lake Superior. Some find even greater strength by being attuned with nature's elders and are blessed all the more. In whatever forms, at whatever times and places available, find the elders waiting to help you. The benefits are manifold.

Arnold Mindell in his brilliant book *Sitting in the Fire* [19] makes these experienced observations in relation to being an elder. Something to reflect on:

- The leader follows Robert's Rules of Order; the elder obeys the spirit.
- The leader sees trouble and tries to stop it; the elder sees the troublemaker as a possible teacher.
- The leader strives to be honest; the elder tries to show truth in everything.
- The democratic leader supports democracy; the elder does this, too, but also listens to dictators and ghosts.
- Leaders try to be better at their jobs; elders try to get others to become elders.
- Leaders try to be wise; elders have no minds of their own. They follow the events of nature.

- The leader needs time to reflect; the elder takes only a moment to notice what's happening.
- The leader knows; the elder learns.
- The leader tries to act; the elder lets things be.
- The leader needs a strategy; the elder studies the moment.
- The leader follows a plan; the elder honors the direction of a mysterious and unknown river.

To ENTER A DISCUSSION OF BELIEF REQUIRES A CERTAIN REFITTING, a change of equipment and tools that allows new ways of sensing to emerge. One of the helpful elements is some kind of personal permeability that can hear the other elements and let in the voices of nature and spirit. Some may call it God. This allows one to be touched, to join in dialogue with the universal forces where the larger soul resides. To believe is to trust in mystery, in the nebulous images moving in undifferentiated space—and to imagine them as helpful and supportive. Prayer then is a tool that makes entering the unknown possible. Prayer calls in our support, connects us with our deeper selves, our communities and heritage, and our ability to choose, in part, the direction of our evolution.

I can almost feel people cringe as they read this, just as I have watched men in hundreds of circles shrink, or expand with hostility, at the mention of prayer. Many men and women have been misled by the proponents of prayer in all religions. It may be more a matter of misunderstanding the magnitude of prayer than anything else. The word itself has become synonymous with abandoned passion. Too often the methodology of prayer has prescribed a limited approach motivated by the promise of heaven or the threat of hell. Individual expression is sublimated to the correct way, the only way to save one's soul. Inner wisdom and soul direction are often left out. For the people who have fled from such oppressive practices, prayer has become a dirty word. I'm afraid the old saying about throwing the baby out with the bath water applies here. To me, prayer is the baby, the precious essence of religion, simple, personal, alive, growing, inquisitive. I wish to help people take it back for themselves, for their people, and for the earth. Otherwise, I fear, we will not have the tools in our knapsacks necessary for the exploration of mystery and faith, so essential to the survival of our soul lives.

It gets back to the metaphor of the tundra. Diversity is its strength. For those who match up well with organized religion, the tundra welcomes them. Again, as the elder said, we don't need fewer religions, or just the right ones. We need all of the religions, all of the approaches, more and new and different ones rising up in mushroom glory from the dormant spores of yearning. It is the yearning, in the words of Michael Meade, that connects us to God. What is needed are more avenues of connection to spirit, to the spirit yearning that unites all people. Men yearn for more access to meaning, to that which inspires, to the ways of heart and beauty.

There's a northern Mexico First Nation People prayer, from the Yaqui, that puts it all together: I am another you, you are another me.

I'm not here to pit one approach against another. I feel responsible, however, to support the rights of those subjected to a one-God-one-way-to-freedom approach. It has never made sense to me—and many of the men I have worked with—to present a dogmatic, limited, exclusionary belief system. In my experience, these ways often bring about rote, semi-conscious responses from the followers. Life's initiations require more of us.

All religions serve as mythic containers, created originally thousands of years ago to help us mature into a path with heart and soul, inspired by spirit. If the container, the teachings and practice are not flexible, are incapable of growing along with our evolving souls, people become disillusioned, cut off from their own spiritual powers. In such a state, it is difficult, if not impossible, to find meaning. The world elders teach that to be engaged in personal and community meaning is the central task of life. To live from meaning, spread and share it with our people, is another form of the wild tundra flower that releases its beautiful scent to the wind.

I continue to advocate taking back prayer and the tending of soul as an individual practice. We are diminished, I believe, when we give that power completely to intercessors and expect them to take care of it. It's one thing to actively pray in a strong spiritual community. I don't mean to discount its power and beauty. My concern is when people give away their meaning to something outside themselves, seen as better than they are, and in time feel empty. It seems many of us in modern life give ourselves away to the great religions, or any spiritual practice, and in doing so lose some of its originally intended meaning. The pervasive apathy in our culture is a sign, clear and palpable to anyone who cares to notice, that our soul waters are not being replenished. Like the aquifers of the Great Plains, the water is drying up, much of the American dream, the parts that do not sustain the human soul, are coming unmasked as a hoax, and something's got to give.

My suggestion is an old and common one, a simple standby that has served humanity for eons. Faith. Return to faith and the meaning of blood and ancestry. Find something to believe in that is greater than ourselves. Serve. Have faith and believe that to serve Spirit, God, Allah, is to answer the deepest calling. Take the risk to enter mystery, and find the tools and support, that make entry possible. Everywhere I look, men and women are finding a way out of the flatness and half life of an indifferent world. Real warmth awaits the pilgrims of this land, a way out of depression, addiction, misery, violence and isolation. Each of us already knows the way to our meaning, our purpose and fulfillment and the grace of living in our passion and power. I don't know the best way for anyone but myself; even then the road is often difficult. I know how impossible it appears at times. The echoes of the old ones reach us and say, "Find your way, start to open up, inquire, feel the longing and sadness, and take the risk to believe." This is the way to replenish the soul aquifer. It is somewhat of a paradox, but it seems we replenish the waters by drinking from them. Often this filling happens in the soul crafts practiced in responsible communities.

I am recalled again to the words of the medicine man who asked me, "What stops you from being the man you have come to be in this lifetime?" It surely isn't the biology that stops me. Being alive in the growing environment of my own cells regenerating themselves, constantly striving to survive, driven to build muscle onto bone, to eat and drink, however possible, tells me the biology has no doubt about its purpose. The flesh knows the ancestral and collective wisdom, accumulated through the seasons one upon the other. Something else stops me.

Somewhere inside of me dwells the force of disconnection. For reasons, lots of reasons, I stop myself. And so a part of my prayer life seeks to find and work with the barriers to my self expression. I want to return myself to the soil of the forest floor that invites so many ways to grow. I seek the elements that allow freedom. This is the nature that finds ways through barriers, that is able to bless who we are, and fill us with the grace to bless those who come after us. What else besides faith would encourage the pine cone to let go of its parent tree or the acorn to free fall from the oak? It is built into the genetic code. Something that says, Yes, go for it, take the risk, leap into the unknown.

I heard a story from a story teller that illustrates this idea. He spoke of a man teaching rock climbing to a small group of adults. He was exhibiting techniques against a rock face, and had reached the top of a seventy-five-foot escarpment, free climbing with no ropes. In that instant, he slipped. Instead of falling, he pushed himself against the rock wall, with all his strength, and sprang away from the wall. Within seconds, he found himself crashing through the branches of a tree. He hit the ground, conscious, with only minor injuries. He looked at himself, as if to ask what life he had fallen into. The gaping mouths of his students expressed the same wonder. Was it faith that inspired him to leap, somehow knowing, or remembering, the tree was there? Perhaps it is true that living out of faith requires more than a little foolishness.

It's interesting to me to consider stories like this, of critical times when assertive faith saves one's life. There are many more instances of this than we realize, when a decision taken or not taken alters our lives. I want to know what stops us from living in this boldness on a daily basis, and from learning to recognize the importance of what we do. What keeps us from growing up and standing tall in the forest and the city streets, and welcoming the storms of winter, the lightning and thunder of summer, while we protect and shelter the young and the elderly? I don't think there is a shortage of mythology. We still know the stories of human experience passed on for thousands of years. Our living elders and nature itself bring life forward and inform us of our potential. There are no easy answers as to why it is so difficult to embrace the sources of inspiration available to us. Maybe the answer is not the goal. I simply encourage the exploration of such questions and find the inquiry itself, similar to the yearning, to be profound in its own way. Again, paradox: the question is the answer.

One way or another, in some form, manifestation, or shape, the thread of truth that runs through these questions is belief. How do we find the ability or learn to believe in ourselves, our blood line, in all of humanity's potential? How do we sustain such beliefs in the face of unexpected failures and disappointments? I don't imagine there are complete answers to these questions. Whatever insights that come would likely be partially inexpressible. Again, one word in our language comes close to the matter: faith. Faith is the living component of belief. If belief is the trunk of the tree, faith is the sap running between the bark and the trunk. Faith bleeds when a blow is stricken with an ax, and it is also the scar tissue that forms to stop the bleeding. Faith lies underground through the long winter with the promise to rise again from dormancy with the juice to feed new blooms. Faith does not rest on logical proof or material evidence. It is a knowing that transcends circumstance.

To claim our places in the continuum of human evolution and contribute to the work our ancestors began so long ago, we must believe in the importance of our part, to consciously take on the practice of trusting ourselves and our communities, to sustain ourselves with faith, and then find ways to sustain our faith. Once again, it is prayer that comes to mind.

Every time I mention the word prayer, I am reminded of the reactions it gets when I bring it up at the men's retreats I guide. We've already covered the terrain of betrayal and shame that many associate with prayer. Because it is so loaded and edgy for so many of us, I believe prayer needs to be redefined. The standard definition says that prayers are written in books and must be said certain ways at certain times only. This does not serve. The Lakota medicine man, Fools Crow, quoted in the introduction, talks about the difficulty his people had with such an approach to prayer. What keeps showing up at all the retreats is this definition of prayer:

> Prayer is anything that connects us to meaning, that helps us believe
> in ourselves and our purposes, that sustains a faith in life and

nature, that connects us to our blood lineage, our children, elders, partners and communities; anything that serves in this way is prayer, is sacred, beloved and full of grace.

Despite the connotation prayer has for many people, there are countless manifestations of prayerful ways in modern life. I support all of these, individual and organized, that make time for soul matters. Our contemporary civilization moves faster and faster, and it seems there is less and less time for sacred activities. If, however, we come to understand an expanded definition of prayer, there are more ways to incorporate prayer in our daily lives, and perhaps we can find little openings that can be dripped into with the flow of simple, conscious, prayerful acts, that will in time—like frost shattering or erosion—open these little gaps into great cathedrals. The flow I'm referring to is fed by reverence, a conscious softening of one's preferences, troubles, ambitions, confusion and choosing to respect, deeply, whatever is before us. This is the essence of ritual, and ritual is the well that is filled by us drinking from it. Reverence leads to surrender, the owning of judgments, easing control, the will to have it our way. Reverence, surrender, letting go, open a gateway to respect, and in a reverential and respectful awareness, guidance becomes possible.

Prayer becomes a conduit, a channel, an open window to energy that can move through in unexpected ways. Prayer connects us to the past, present and future meaning of life, the vast nondenominational pool of soul. We talk about sustainable culture, sustainable business, sustainable housing and so on. Soul is what sustains. If we do not draw on the pool of soul that is filled by our drinking, nothing will last.

Since boyhood I have witnessed countless men pray. I have always been fascinated by the magic of it. I remember being an altar boy at my first high Catholic mass in Latin. The priest wore the full vestments, and we altar boys wore our cassocks. We processed down the main isle of the cathedral, the altar boys preceding the priest, who carried the scepter. We walked up and stopped at the three steps up to the massive altar. The Ten Commandments were inscribed on great pillars. The sense of reverence was terrifying. We would go to our knees and bow to the altar with our hands clasped to our chests and say the long opening prayer in Latin. The whole church waited for this prayer to open the mass. The power of it moved me, and began a lifelong fascination with the many faces of prayer.

Perhaps it is by my attentions to the ceremony that I have been able to perceive the deepening and timelessness it brings to the practitioners. I have noticed that after men pray they are strengthened, more confident and compassionate. They seem to be expanded in some way, more capable of holding larger questions, contradictions, conflict, which might otherwise lead to shutting down or lashing out. At times prayer makes men more crazy, and this is of great importance for a man who is sorting out his anger and frustrations. More mystery can inspire them and intuitive guidance can emerge. They reconnect to their personal faith, the strong foundation from which meaning and purpose can spring . From this comes a true sense of identity, the experience of self and authenticity. What I have noticed is that the form doesn't seem to matter. Men reach these places of personal depth and discovery not by doing it right or a certain way or by exactly following the footsteps of a master. They arrive by living in their own questions, joining with their own yearning and expressing it in their prayers, rituals, stories and lives. When this part of the psyche is palpated, it comes alive. Thus, the questions and yearning can stay healthy and can grow. It's like exercising a muscle.

One of the important personal openings to this teaching came to me in my thirties. My yearning informed me of a desire for guidance and the need to complete some confused and broken experiences left over from my twenties. In moments of silence I openly called for support and found myself returning to the land where I had spent most of my twenties—the upper peninsula of Michigan and the shores of Lake Superior. Shortly after arriving in Marquette, Michigan, I bumped into an old friend and elder, Hilda Rasmussen. Hilda invited me to come with her the next day to visit a friend in Munsing. I agreed to go and immediately felt my body react with a vibrating, anxious sensation.

We drove together along the shoreline of Lake Superior. The power of the lake as a great natural force added to the anxiety in my body. We drove into Munising, an old fishing village and formerly a lumber mill that supplied frames for Model T's in the early 1900s. The house of Hilda's friend was a simple structure, but the minute we walked in I was hit with the scent of something true, the smell of evolved eldership. At the head of the dining room table sat Alice Treadway. In that moment, when our eyes met, something happened in the room. A silent, reverent energy, charged and condensed, overwhelmed me. Upon later reflection, I came to see it as a fluctuation in time that transported me into a largeness or compression that shaped lifetimes into moments. I was not afraid. After a short while, I returned to normal experience as if falling through many levels of reality to the earth, and landing in a realm of pure love. All of this had happened during introductions.

I knew intuitively that I belonged nowhere else but here, with this woman. A part of me that had lived long ago, that had known and embodied a deep, profound way of living had been contacted. My meeting Alice Treadway brought this awareness to me instantly. I had heard of her when I lived in Marquette those many years ago, but I was not ready then. She had the reputation as a tough medicine woman who had been helping people find their meaning and purpose for most of her seventy-some years. In her medicine work she helped people align themselves with their personal life destiny. Her upbringing involved wild crafting and foraging for food in the forest. Her family lived in a small cabin and heated with wood. Most of her time had been in the outdoors. In her mid-thirties she received a series of explicit dreams that she resisted for many years. The dreams, as she described them, had the vividness of waking consciousness. She could literally hear and taste and see the full range of color and touch as if she were physically experiencing the dreams. The dreams told of a shamanic practice that wanted her to bring it forth as a way to guide people into soul evolution. Alice called the method "The 29 Steps to Godhood." She believed each of us had come to life many times, over and over, on our path to Godhood, or what she called evolved humanhood that endears us to divine compassion and love.

We spent the day telling stories and partook in a healing prayer circle that had been part of Alice's practice all of her life. I gave Alice a massage, having completed a program in massage therapy. When Hilda and

I stood to leave, Alice looked at me with her mostly blind eyes and said, "Come back and work with me." It was a clear invitation, the significant moment my body had prepared me for earlier. It took five months for me to arrange another visit. In the depth of winter I returned and spent twelve days alone with Alice Treadway. We worked every day. A morning session and an afternoon session. She put me through her forum. I have pages of notes from this compressed time with her that packed, in a few days, years of teaching. The details are less important. The essence is. Alice Treadway helped me reconnect to my spiritual, soul support system, something I had once known and operated out of but had mostly lost. Alice called it, "Having your team."

She would sit in front of her fireplace at the beginning of each session and ask the question, "Who are we working with today?" She always lined up her team, never worked without first assembling her soul support. Then she looked at me, or more correctly, sensed me, given her state of near blindness, and asked out loud, "And who is Jeffrey's team? Who are his helpers?" In silence next to the fire's radiance, we waited. Then again Alice asked me directly, "Who is on your team?" Images, entities, archetypes, beings, spirits, whatever they wished to be called began showing up. These helpers were the team that would always be with me and help me through the challenges and difficulties of my life. She taught me that Spirit, at least in part, is there to assist us in finding our meaning, purpose and loving. She was strong about asking for the team to show up, and giving thanks to it when it departed.

She had a unique perception of Spirit and the spirit team that assembled for any given period. Things would be going along, apparently quite well, and she would suddenly say, "Okay, we're done. Spirit has left." And that was it. Or she would say, "Our team is gone," and we would end the session. Often, the factors that most contributed to her saying this appeared related to the level of ego present. As soon as someone began to think it was he or she, and become attached to his part in the healing or insight, Alice could sense the way it squeezed out Spirit.

It's strange to consider that, as much as she touched me, I still resist her teaching at times. I forget—which is one of the most common forms of resistance—and let myself drift without inviting my team to support me. Having experienced the fullness and peace of the team, it is amazing that I would ever leave it behind, but that is what happens. And so I have often said, as much to myself as to anyone else, that a prayerful life, or a life of faith, is a process of remembering, and often remembering to remember. It is a practice of developing second sight, as the shaman have described it, that nudges us back to the awareness of our sacred truth. It's almost as if a member of our team, or maybe several, are given permission, or asked, or assigned the job of reminding us. They might say to us, Remember what you said? Remember who you found yourself to be that time in the sweat bath, or when you heard the poet read, or that moment in a particular dance when a vision came to you, or the wisdom of the desert during a solo fast? This prodding to recall who we are, to renew the practices that feed our yearning and connect us to our meaning, is to me the essence of a soulful path. I like the way William Stafford speaks of it in his poem, *A Ritual to Read to Each Other*:

> *If you don't know the kind of person I am*
> *and I don't know the kind of person you are*
> *a pattern that others made may prevail in the world*
> *and following the wrong god home we may miss our star.*

> *For there is many a small betrayal in the mind,*
> *a shrug that lets the fragile sequence break*
> *sending with shouts the horrible errors of childhood*
> *storming out to play through the broken dike.*

> *And as elephants parade holding each elephant's tail,*
> *but if one wanders the circus won't find the park,*
> *I call it cruel and maybe the root of all cruelty*
> *to know what occurs but not recognize the fact.*

> *And so I appeal to a voice, to something shadowy,*
> *a remote important region in all who talk:*
> *though we could fool each other, we should consider—*
> *lest the parade of our mutual life get lost in the dark.*

For it is important that awake people be awake,
or a breaking line may discourage them back to sleep;
the signals we give—yes or no, or maybe—
should be clear: the darkness around us is deep. [20]

And so once again I am reminded to remember to stay awake to my soul team, to remain conscious of my teachers, my elders and my ancestors, lest I find myself following the wrong god home. In considering the reasons I fall asleep to my wisdom, it often rests on fear. I might prefer to believe it is a fear that I am not good enough, but perhaps it is more often the fear Nelson Mandela spoke of in his inaugural address, quoting from a poem by Mary Anne Williamson.[21] "Our deepest fear is not that we are inadequate. Our deepest fear is that we are powerful beyond measure. It is our light, not our darkness, that most frightens us." We hold ourselves back because who we truly are frightens us. What we may be asked to do, the ways in which we can contribute to life if we are to truly come alive, sometimes contrasts sharply with the self judgments of who we conceive ourselves to be. When we identify with judgments diminishing our worth, and imagine it is the problem, the power of that voice holds us back. Perhaps it is more true that the smallness is a reaction to our greatness, to the very greatness of God and nature, and that we shield ourselves from it by identifying with the victim. Look what was done to me. Look at how I was abused or abandoned or betrayed. *This* is why I am small, and must remain so, because of how grievously I have been wounded. When in fact, our greatness knows these wounds are like arrows shot into a young cottonwood, so easily grown over and embedded in heartwood that welcomes conversation with the intruders. Wounds are not excuses. They often turn out to be the pathways to heart and soul evolution. When we survive the wounding, it speaks to our greatness, and the reasons to stay awake, to continue holding the tail of the elephant in front of us, so that we can all move forward. Greatness is very normal. It is often quiet. It is not about dominion over others, over the earth. Greatness is about losing ourselves in the wounds of all nature, and coming to rest on the true virtues of love. As Mozart said:

Neither a lofty degree of intelligence nor imagination nor both together go into the making of genius. Love, love, love, that is the soul of genius.

Alice Treadway was blind, but she held the tails of her ancestors and invited others to find their meaning by grasping with their trunks her strong tail. She gave of herself fully and did not allow false fears to diminish her contribution. She knew and lived the genius of which Mozart spoke.

What stops me from remembering and disconnects me from meaning and purpose is when I lose faith and start to believe it doesn't matter. When I allow myself to become withdrawn and imagine I can do nothing about whatever it is that troubles me, then I fall asleep. Then, when the satellite dish salesman comes to the door with a special introductory offer, I say, Okay, what the hell. I stop caring and fall into unconsciousness. Then it is the holy craziness of this helpless place, almost killing me, with which I must contend. Gratefully, there is a remembering at these times—that can only come out of this despairing place. It is the greatness of my ancestors that calls me to stay awake, to continue believing, and praying, and dancing, and making rituals of the simple tasks that face me. I am not enrolled in the cultural myth that equates greatness with fame. This is not about impressing others or seeing one's name in lights. Those that shape culture and the evolution of the human heart are most often people who are not famous, wealthy, popular or attractive. They are people who have learned how to forgive, themselves and others, and have decided that, despite everything, they will work in their homes, communities, churches, pagan circles, wherever they are called, because, as William Stafford says, "It is important that awake people be awake…the darkness around us is deep."

Faith and the belief in self, and the subsequent respect in others, does not play like the march of a brass band. In these times of fast cut digital imagery and Dolby surround sound, computer-animated special effects and all the whiz bang techno-magic, it is easy to miss the subtle, gentle ways of flowing in the simple, relaxed currents of faith and prayer. Entertainment and the lavish ego prancing dramas have an element of fun that serves an important purpose. Nonetheless, in our final breath, the satisfaction that will have made our lives worthwhile probably won't come from such pursuits. At least that is what I've gathered from studying and spending time with those making the passage into death. What they tell me, or what I remember, is that the times of wakefulness, of full and conscious living, often in simple moments with children or nature, are the soul truths that make it all worthwhile, and provide some sense of legacy, a carrying forward of the ancestral soul and a passing on of nourishment to the future soul.

I remember a young man named Alberto Rivera, from Manhattan, who came to a camp one time. He is a young rap poet who reminded me of myself the first time I had come into a circle of men to pray, to heal, to envision, and to find myself. Alberto brought a fire, a passion, a caution, a concern for people his age and all humanity. I watched him closely for three days. He was filled by the grace of being seen in the way only old men could see him. And I watched them equally fill, become more vibrant and alive with what he brought to them. At the end of our time together—as is the usual practice—we completed our experience in a brief summary called "checking out." Alberto stepped up, in a room that had come to love him for his questions, his beauty, his struggle, and shifted into his rap poet handle The U.S. (The Universal Solution). His body softened into waves of movement, and in a flurry of well-articulated language, he pulled in images from the whole three days. He danced them and rhymed them and returned them to all of us.

It was an instantaneous work of art, not held to any canvas or medium, but meant to pass away as fast as it came. It left us all breathless, touched by some kind of profound care and love. There was something about this young man, and the eighty-six-year-old elder who witnessed him, that created a broad range where all of us could find ourselves, and place ourselves in the power of who we are. Alberto gave of his talent, opened himself up (as so many of the men do at our gatherings) and reached us, in a way I will never forget.

And so the circle comes around again to the questions: Who is your soul team? How do you remember them and ask for assistance on a path of meaning and purpose? How does this team support you in your beauty and give you the strength to support and serve your family and community, the earth around and beneath you? In what ways can you work with your soul team to build a flourishing village that sustains even after you are gone? When you are really down, gasping for air, not sure if you can live another day, bucking from the demands of life, is there a way you can love, honor or bless the part of you that hurts so much, and yet continues to care so deeply? Having this kind of self compassion is a way that can help sort out the crazy times and keep us alive.

There are many ways to deepen these questions and condition ourselves to receive the subtle, intuitive guidance of the team. Go into nature and let the wisdom of the seasons hold you in the questions. Create a circle of friends and work in contemplative silence. Light candles and ask, "Who is my team?" Ask that unwanted energies, like false fear, worry, constricting self doubt, be cleared so that Spirit guides, your team, your helpers may be present. Open your body to what shows up. When it appears that some sort of support has come in, some image, perhaps a grandparent, a hawk or a bear, a biblical prophet or beautiful waterfall, ask, "Are you one of my helpers?" Ask three times. If no response comes, then whatever appeared is probably not part of your team. If something comes that shows its teeth to you in a threatening manner, it's usually a good idea to assertively ask it to leave. Your team may also be found in a sound, a rhythm, a small warmth in your body. Only you can determine who makes up your team.

As you become familiar with your team, eventually they can become part of daily life. In the morning, for example, ask the questions, "Who is my team today? Who is working, supporting and guiding me?" The team may not come all at once. Some days there may be only one team member present. Other days, five or more may arrive. In my experience, whoever or whatever shows up is very real and alive. The team exists and has a physical presence, similar in some ways to light, which we can only see in a very small range of its spectrum, yet we know the physical power of the invisible spectrum in the form of X-ray, infrared, short-wave and microwave. Still, perhaps it is a stretch to conceive of a spirit team as physically real. It may come across as animism, superstition or an occult practice. It seems to me, however, there is no shortage of such conceptions in all of the great religions. Christianity has its angels, Buddhism its guardians and demons, Hinduism its pantheon, Taoism its nature spirits. We fundamentally understand the truth of a spirit world that runs parallel to our own. It troubles me that logical thinking and the narrow range of this modality should cut us off from other realities that can so enrich our lives. To me, logical thought is like the visible light spectrum. It represents one small section of the full wave, at best only one quarter of the whole being. To imagine it is the only truth, to let it dominate so as to squeeze out other—not just possibilities—realities, would be something like cutting off one's arms and legs because the heart cannot be heard beating in them. Calling on the spirit team requires to some degree a surrender of the logical mind, a giving up of that grasping, confining consciousness. It is a step into mystery. What shows up is sometimes not what you would have wished for. The spirit team, linked with the soul circle, has a view on our lives that may be quite different from what we believe is true, or from what we might want. Opening up to this wisdom will be surprising, frightening, sad, educational, joyful. It is important to cultivate an attitude of gratitude, to give thanks for whatever shows up, even if it brings difficulty.

It is important to remember, in all circumstances, the spirit team of the true human heart never subscribes to acts of violence, dominion, or self importance over another human or the earth. Although it is possible to misuse the powers of a spirit team, whenever it is done the result breaks down our human dream. One of the ways we stay awake, as one poet suggests, is to watch for these misuses—in ourselves as well as others—and keep our purposes true.

Another way to engage the spirit team in daily life is through invocation. There may be a project or activity that would be served by increased guidance or support. A physical ritual or prayer, intentionally carried out, can serve to call in the guidance. The speaking or physical activity of ritual opens the gateway. Somehow, simply thinking these things isn't enough. The team wants us to do something, to show with a real, demonstrable action that we are sincere about the request. Simple things like lighting a candle, taking a listening prayer walk, speaking an invocation into nature, finding a place of solitude and quiet to work in and to listen from—all of these and many others serve the purpose. If, for some reason, during such practice it does not feel like the spirit team comes in, ask yourself the question, "What blocks me?" Bless this and send it on its way. Acknowledge the blockage, honor it, understand that it too serves, and ask it to leave. Sometimes this may take some time, an effort toward listening to the blockage, understanding what it represents, why it exists. It may require negotiating with the blockage, as with a young child, promising not to take any risks that will unnecessarily endanger it. There are many ways to work with the blockages. Whatever you do, whether it's exercise, steam baths, sauna sweats, massage, the key factor is the honoring. If blockages and resistance aren't held as sacred, if they are reviled or despised, they become more entrenched, more powerful and capable of subverting our purpose. They cannot be wished away or pushed away. They exist for very good reasons—and, ultimately, even if they appear to be our enemies, to limit and prevent us from advancing. Underneath it all, they too are part of our team and want a good life for us.

To miss this is to risk becoming rigid, holding again to the small spectrum of visible light and being dominated by logical thinking, judgments and prejudice. The expectation that we can will our way through blockages, hesitations or fears leaves little room for love and grace and serendipity. Some kind of letting go, of dying to a long held way of life and inviting to the table a limitation we have battled our whole lives, makes it possible to receive the blessings and support we have craved all along. Once again, paradox dances at the edge of the fire light. Never have I met a man or a woman excluded from this human struggle, both internal and external. This is the rendering that brings out the soul's strength.

Time and time again I have seen and learned from my elders and the men and women I have served the untold beauty of surrendering to the sacred ways of mystery. When people seek contemplative openness, when they open the gateway through prayer, bless and honor their resistance and release it, give up the need for answers, solutions, reasons, a profound grace fills their bodies. Pathways and guidance come rushing in. Healing, love, beauty, wonder and meaning come rushing in. I don't know how all of the people I have worked with arrive at these blessed intersections. Each has blood wisdom that confounds analysis. What I perceive is something holy, something waiting, eternal, wise in the unity of timeless humanity, ready to help each and every one of us. It is simply true that regardless of race, religion or social status a vast potential of spirit and soul wealth awaits our yearning with a warm blanket and a hot bowl of soup. The things that bring meaning and love hold a place in the circle for us. I cannot live in the abandoned, victimized consciousness that says we have lost such beauty. The thread has not been broken, and so I plead with all my heart that the awake people, those who hear the call even faintly, begin to work with their spirit teams. Identify a practice, some way of connecting with the ever-flowing stream of soul, kindness and nature that awaits us so tenderly. And at times it waits not so tenderly.

What this looks like is beyond any framework I might lay out. Prayer is like the Tao, any attempt to define it is not it. And yet, as Lao Tzu says, there are certain properties and elemental components that can be described. Prayer lives. It moves in a fluid dimension that can come to stillness at any time and mirror our longings. It washes as the spring creek over the green mossy rock. It takes us to the center, where awareness of choices, genuine possibilities, show us their wares. It introduces us to our ancestors and our heritage of allies. It does not respond to dogma, one-way-only preferences, institutional authority, guru mandates or idolatry. It calls us to choose our spiritual destinies.

I truly believe in the heart and soul of humanity. If we accept responsibility for our evolution and growth, it is possible to know love, forgiveness and joy, and be a force for peace in our communities and the world. We will not follow false gods home. We will recognize dogma, dominance, prejudice, hatred, oppression—both in our own belief systems and the culture around us. In the regular practice of spiritual devotion, in whatever form, the ground of meaning will be rich, ever present to draw from, so that we may each grow and blossom. Our children and all of the people will be left with good soil in which to root, and the earth itself will sigh and give thanks that we have lived.

I REMEMBER A TIME WHEN AN ELDER OF MINE SAT ME DOWN AND said, "Your preferences are your prisons…and you must have them." Out of this paradox, a question arises for me as I navigate through each day: How do I deal with the body-splitting paradox of preferences when they lead to projections about culture, about others, about myself and the secrets that will never be told? This question, in the context of prayer, meaning and ritual, inevitably draws down into the unknown places in my psyche the raw and primitive energies that call to be mined and rendered into consciousness. These energies are quite often unwelcome in me. I would rather not have them. They aren't laudable, exemplary or heroic. I would rather project them onto some despicable character *out there*, and complain about the terrible things it does. The attempt to work with and integrate such unwelcome energies, to take them back, claim them as my own and be responsible for them, gives rise to another paradox: That which I struggle with or fear about myself can become a great gift. It becomes like a reserve of energy freed up, a source that pushes the raw material of the psyche into form and meaning. There is an old French saying: The cure for the pain is in the pain.

I have witnessed many times the transformations of this process. Elders and teachers, such as Tom Daly, have refined a form of this work the creators call Shadow Dance®. It is a pan-cultural form drawn from several healing traditions. This vital and dynamic practice of dancing shadow characters, bringing out disowned, disliked, generally "dissed" aspects of the self, and witnessing others doing the same, has made clear the paradox of beauty rising from the muck. Others who have shared their wisdom in a similar manner include a seventy-five-year-old elder, Airic Leonardson, who has traveled fifty-five years studying the human soul and serving humanity with what he has learned. Of course there are also many wonderful books, such as Robert Johnson's *Owning Your Own Shadow*,[22] and Robert Bly's *The Little Book on the Human Shadow*,[23] as well as the pioneering work of Carl Jung. I would not venture to present a definitive study of such matters, only to illuminate through my own experience the wisdom of my teachers, and perhaps further the study and practice of such a valuable form.

The importance of paradox has been known for a long time. All sides of the human psyche call out to be expressed and acted upon. This simply means addressed in the inner workings of one's being with the help of elders and community. No doubt our ancestors found themselves in prayer and ceremonial practices that allowed for a metaphorical expression—in physical ways—of the so-called human evils. They knew how to set up safe ritual containers for these expressions. These spiritual communities from around the world have been doing their soul evolution work for thousands of years. Theirs is the very inspiration that feeds the hopes of the future.

It strikes me that a large portion of our culture is conversant in psychological terminology. People understand something of the unconscious, and accept, to some degree, the idea of forces at play within themselves they aren't entirely aware of. The process (begun in childhood) of stuffing feelings and hiding aspects of who we are from parents, teachers and religious leaders so as to avoid pain and ridicule, is a common theme in art, literature and popular non-fiction writing. I'm not sure if it's quite as well understood how to bring these shadow parts into consciousness before they play out in acts of violence, jealousy, masochism, addiction, envy, hatred, bigotry, and on and on. We don't seem to be as well equipped at mining these nuggets of gold left for us by our ancestors. The energies to which I speak lie undigested in our bodies, capable in such a coagulated state to gather up and lash out suddenly at our children, lovers, and the contradictions our modern world presents us each day.

In the many hundreds of circles in which I have sat, with men, women, youth and elders, I have learned that the ability to be compassionate, to love and accept others and have tolerance for differences comes directly from an embrace of the shadow side within ourselves. It is through the work of setting free these trapped energies—in appropriate containers, such as ritual that is held and witnessed as sacred (this is essential)—that people learn to own their judgments and see that they too make mistakes and are capable of hurting others. To see that what they despise in others is more than likely something they despise in themselves. It has become clear in my work supporting people in ritual initiations and transitions that none of us, no matter how good our childhood, has escaped the innocent, automatic wounding and fracturing of our souls. Through the process of acculturation, we all have monsters and angels stuffed in the nuclear powerhouse of the unknown, unconscious being. The ancient peoples understood this and constantly worked with these powers. The process of maturation is largely a rebirthing of the unconscious forces through ritual and prayer—a kind of re-awakening process into an adult framework.

There is a big difference between opinion and projection. An opinion may be held in a manner less charged, less certain of its validity, more in the spirit of healthy debate and inquiry. A projection, because it is so real—literally an image we see in full color, put upon another—has a destructive potential and can serve as the basis of untold atrocities. If it is not reclaimed and seen as the manifestation of an internal struggle, its object can easily be made an enemy that deserves to be punished. The longer these trapped energies are ignored, the greater their power over us, and the more dangerous they become to ourselves, our families and communities. I am convinced it is unintegrated and trapped soul energies that allow us to destroy the environment. The longer we ignore these deep powers, the harder we have to work to keep ourselves asleep and anesthetized in order to prevent unpleasant eruptions—and still they come. We wring our hands and say something has to be done about the violence, but by and large we still refuse to repatriate our banished monsters and accept that the most horrible acts are committed by people no different than ourselves.

A great example of this is the recent apology of Pope John Paul. By publicly acknowledging the church's participation in violence, prejudice and spiritual exclusivity, he took back these projected beliefs and claimed them as something the church needed to work on, to heal and to change. It was an act of honesty and courage that brought a degree of soul-truth back into the faith. It was a relief to witness an institution of such magnitude begin to come to terms with its past. All of the followers, and in many ways the people of the world, gained a direct experience of what it means to embrace our shadows by the example of this powerful elder.

To one degree or another, all of us undergo something similar in the initiations of our lives. The process of being born into innocence, then being defeated by our own families, schools, churches, institutions and nature itself is the holy paradox we are given as human beings. It is our threshing, unavoidable in the harvest of being alive, and yet it is so easy to forget to lean down and gather the grain. These are the seeds of vision and adult inspiration that can sustain a life of meaning and purpose. Indigenous people knew this and continually went into the dark places to gather the seeds of meaning from the holy paradox. We too, in our blood line, carry the passed on shadow material. In some sense, we also receive the understanding of its value.

Robert Bly, in *A Little Book on the Human Shadow*, speaks of the cutting down to size that happens to all people: the passage from pure innocence into a diminished state required of us by culture. Mr. Bly and others make it clear the necessity of this process. They do not, however, condone a lifetime of avoiding our shadow aspects and projecting them onto others with overcharged hatred, envy or bitterness. They instead call us to the work of reclaiming: the hard, hot, sweaty effort of rendering the old carcasses into a fluid, life-enhancing form. Through contact with elders, nature and solitude we are challenged to mine the gold trapped in the deeply buried treasure houses of youth. The fact that it's trapped down there is not to be avoided. Parents who imagine they won't do this to their children are fooling themselves. It has to happen, simply because we want certain standards of civility and discipline from our children that often go against their primitive urges. In order to survive, and receive the absolutely essential approval of their parents, children comply with what is being asked of them. The approval they gain through self-denial is sometimes the only recognition children receive, and becomes for them the very breath of their survival. Many of us grow up believing the only way to receive love is through self-neglect and conformity to the standards of our families. Some hollow ringing calls to us from the interior, as an empty cask of wine pounded on by a wooden hammer, begging us to open the valves to a new vintage.

Now the task is to approach those defeating experiences in a spiritual framework, to turn them into stories and rituals and prayers. Putting the story into the container of awareness and prayer, like yeast in a vat of grape juice, can begin a transformation. I have witnessed the process in the work of hundreds of men. They go in as soul biologists to dissect and probe their inner make up and pull out the pieces of who they really are—not the personality or self-image they would prefer to be associated with, but the true knobby, grizzly, twisted, bloody components that allow a being to carry on. They find the stuffed energies of childhood, now grown into spiny trolls and warted vipers, or terribly frightened, dimly lit angels, ancestral deities or artistic geniuses and bring them forward to be seen, honored and placed in respectful seats around the warm soul fire. The healing work is profound, and charged with the unfinished business of generations. The paradox here is how normal a process it is: truly humbling, simple and common to all humanity.

Once, in a high country meadow, a man who calls himself Blue Joy a'Singin', felt he had lost the support of his people. With the help of a few elders and his own yearning, we created a ritual in which various men took on the personas of his male lineage, on back into history, generation upon generation. The men stood one behind the next, leading up the hill for nearly a hundred yards. Blue Joy began to see in them the faces of his father—whom he had met once when he was three months old—and his grandfather, great-grandfather and so on. He took his place at the front of the line, and felt them all behind him, all in support of him, caring for him and proud of him. He dropped into a sweet grief realizing they were truly there, had always been there if called upon, and would never abandon him. In this way, the line of power from which he had felt alienated now joined him as part of his spirit team. This is one example among hundreds, in which a man regained his power by integrating his shadows and unknown parts of himself.

I have met with men in snow, hail, gale force winds, blazing sun and the brilliance of every season. We have met at lodges, in teepees, tents, living rooms, basements, garages, conference centers, fields, forests, farms. *It doesn't matter where.* When soulful containers, loved and blessed with prayer, provide ritual space for engaging these lost parts of ourselves, when they are rained on and watered back to life, we are always enriched by them. In some ways, our shadows have been waiting for us to meet them in a conscious way. In so doing, we reclaim ourselves. Our slimy frogs turn into nobleman, our ugly ducklings into swans—or sometimes they stay frogs and ugly ducks that know magic, can read energies, or lay golden eggs.

I do not take this process lightly. It is serious and dangerous work to take up the scalpel and go inside the soul. To ask for time boundaries to drop, to pray for genuine healing, to open the energy reserves in the service of reconstituting shadow parts and plowing them into the psyche all takes a profound dedication and bravery. Any adventure into the spirit world of heart and soul brings with it risk, and should rightfully inspire a healthy fear and caution, and a calling together of the spirit team and allies through prayer. Done thoughtfully, well supported and witnessed, in a blend of biology and spirit, the evolution not just of individuals but of all humanity can be the result. No, I do not take it lightly.

Too many elders and teachers have shown me that we cannot bend the forces of greatness that lie within each of us and mold them into unnatural shapes. Such attempts to dominate inevitably bring harm to us. In a similar vein, guides and facilitators must not foist their own agendas on the people with whom they work. To do so can inflict damage on everyone present. Beware of the facilitator who thinks he knows what's best for you. Chances are he's acting out some old pattern or unactualized inner component *through you* and is not at all able to help you. I consider this a misuse of spirit and prayer. To work without agendas as much as possible often appears to be doing nothing. It is not fancy, impressive or astounding to watch a master work respectfully with the delicate figures of another's soul. I have found, however, that these are truly the ones who can help us change in ways we are ready for and can integrate. The soul is not impressed with pyrotechnics. It likes the quiet play of light in the ripples of a small mountain brook. So too, with inner work I encourage tender, slow but steady exploration. Gentle, persistent, loving. This attentive way of self-kindness shows respect for the mystery.

No matter what the approach or method, paradox arises. Any exploration of the inner dimension brings with it the risk of difficulty, pain, challenge. It would appear easier to go along with the dominant culture and give up on soul matters. And yet, if we stop tending these fires they will go out, and rekindling them is much more difficult than keeping them going, as anyone who has heated with wood will tell you. As it says in the Tao te Ching: the easy way appears difficult and the difficult way appears easy. Each day we are confronted with the question: which way do I go today? Paradox stands as a teacher, whatever our decision. If we are filled with anxiety, the paradox is informing us of stagnation, and nothing can live in stagnant water. In my experience, the difficult way, the paradoxical way, the way of standing in between certainty, between polarity, is the way to a full and diverse life, a life that is compelling and meaningful, a life that can be loved. If we do not love our own lives, how can we care for the children, the elders and the earth itself? And so it comes to us as the holy work of adulthood and maturity to take back the lost treasures of childhood.

To be *aware* of this human journey as we walk through the many passages from birth to death is most of the work. From this humble place of being part of a continuous human endeavor—growing for millions of years toward its own collective heart—is itself the gateway to engage the ancestral spirit. In such a practice, we can find our connections to the ancient human river that flows from each of our contributions. In the drinking from this water of life, from the wisdom of river flowing to sea and the deep undercurrents of the dark waters below, we come to understand the greatness of humanity, to respect it and become its guardians.

Sir Laurens van der Post dedicated his adult life in such a manner to the preservation of the human heart and soul. He describes some of the approach to paradox as, "Integrity to see the feeling and inject the paradox and strive for meaning through an inside personal feeling which in turn moves outside the self." I see him speaking here about being direct and inclusive of the shadow parts of ourselves through prayer, ritual and indigenous wisdom. A Rumi poem describes paradox this way:

> *Night cancels the business of day;*
> *inertia recharges the mind.*
> *Then the day cancels the night,*
> *and inertia disappears in the light.*
> *Though we sleep and rest in the dark,*
> *doesn't the dark contain the water of life?*
> *Be refreshed in the darkness.*
> *Doesn't a moment of silence*
> *restore beauty to the voice?*
> *Opposites manifest through opposites:*
> *in the black core of the heart*
> *God created the eternal light of love.* [24]

The night, which is harder to see, is yet as fully rich with beauty as the day. In modern times there can be a tendency to keep the lights on all night, and to prefer the easy seeing of daytime reality. Again, the paradox. It *seems* easier to look at what appears in the light, to imagine ourselves to be only the parts of ourselves easily seen in the light of waking consciousness. In fact, it is more *difficult* to observe only the light, because it is precisely those less visible elements, those lower and shadowy, that trip us up.

One important teaching of this was the first time I fasted in the desert with only water for four days. Everything around me—the creosote bushes, the lizards, the flies, the occasional bird that appeared so free in spirit—put a mirror to my inner world. After the second day, I was so overwhelmed by seeing the parts of myself that I had discounted and projected on others I could barely stand to be with myself. Having seen parts of who I was in the world for the first time stunned me. By the fourth day I realized there were many bridges I had burned that needed mending, many projections I would slowly begin to pull back in. What I learned from that first time out, and the subsequent solo trips, has been much of my life's work in healing and mending.

It is through the conscious effort to gain awareness of the low and shadowy that the daylight vision gains depth and clarity. Every artist knows about negative space, or shadow, and works with it as much or more than the objects cast in light. One informs the other, gives it depth and meaning, and neither can exist without its counterpart. More often than not, it seems our culture endorses only the light, focuses on the outward appearance of things and often misses the depth available to us by going deeper. D. H. Lawrence wrote:

> I am not a mechanism, an assembly of various sections.
> And it is not because the mechanism is working wrongly, that I am ill,
> I am ill because of wounds to the soul, to the deep emotional self
> and the wounds to the soul take a long, long time, only time can help
> and patience, and a certain difficult repentance
> long, difficult repentance, realization of life's mistake, and the freeing oneself
> from the endless repetition of the mistake
> which mankind at large has chosen to sanctify.[25]

Here are a couple of other pieces of wisdom to chew on about all of this. To quote again from Martin Luther King, "Darkness cannot drive out darkness. Only life can do that. Hate cannot drive out hate. Only love can do that."

Nietzsche said, "Nothing on earth consumes a man more quickly than the passion of resentment."

What I believe these elders and poets are talking about is the grip and destructive force of the human shadow boxed in the psyche. Cut off from the life of the psyche's flow, not having a say or a part in the conscious expression, these shadow aspects become dangerous. They come out in projections, resentment and hatred. Unfortunately, many of the dominant spiritual forms tend not to acknowledge shadow energies within the soul but rather break them out into good and evil, right and wrong dichotomies that do not serve individual growth, and, as an elder said, they must serve a valid purpose or they wouldn't exist. Nonetheless, the one-God-one-way-to-heaven systems can hold people in a form of logical oppression that dampens spirit and hobbles one's ability to question power and be responsible for his own development. Any spiritual system or form needs to learn how to work with the dangers inherent in exclusive devotion. If evil is *out there* and our job is to keep it at bay through the observation of strict codes of behavior, growth is slow and lopsided. The light uninformed by darkness develops a shallow vacuity that is often unsatisfying. The men I have worked with who know this truth still struggle with their own barriers to diving into the banished regions of their beings. Many of us have been so conditioned to desire only the "good," to pursue "happiness" and ease of living. It is also true that we need the resistance to push up against, to make our efforts tangible and our breakthroughs audible. If it were easy, we would be talking about a different sort of journey. This one usually requires prayer and requests for guidance to soften the rigidity of habitual ways of thinking and perceiving the world. I do not think it is possible for a man to approach his own creative connection with the divine on his own. Again, paradox: to achieve solitude we need the support of friends.

I have been watching men's work for fifteen years. There was an initial enthusiasm, large and small gatherings with Robert Bly, Michael Meade, James Hillman, Tom Daly and the like, and then a dropping away. The initial media surge has given way to a more steady and authentic resurgence. Some men have stayed with it the whole time. Others who dropped out because of early roughness and immaturity in the form have returned, and young men continue to arrive with great curiosity and desire. The men I have witnessed continuing this work, persevering and evolving with it, have taken an honorable and very difficult place in the spiritual awakening of modern man. Through Shadow Work® developed by Cliff Barry and Mary Ellen Blandford (see page 181), and Shadow Dance®, developed by Tom Daly and Jude Blitz (see page 181), and influenced by the World Work of Arnie and Amy Mindell, avenues for expressing and integrating shadow parts of the human psyche are alive, functional and quite refined. These people and many of their contemporaries have taken on the task of being helpers in the human soul revolution, teaching responsibility in calling for vision and meaning. Their efforts heal, and return power back to the people's hands.

In the rites of passage course I have co-lead at a local high school with Rachael Kessler,[26] a modern day pioneer in bringing soul back into education, it amazes me to witness young women and men come alive to the possibility of embracing their shadow selves. Rachael has been a pioneer in opening the work of emotional intelligence in our schools. Many of the young people who experience this, like the rest of us, have had to tuck away their unpleasant, primitive urges and desires at a very early age in order to survive. When these energies come out in self-destructive or socially disruptive ways, the young people wonder what's the matter with them. One young woman in particular had a difficult time accepting something about herself she considered a flaw. She grappled with this throughout the course and didn't have it resolved when she "graduated" and was sent into the world. To my surprise and delight, I received a letter from her sometime later describing how she had finally gotten the idea that accepting some perceived flaw in herself was the way to transform it into an asset, and in the process develop a greater appreciation for herself and more tolerance of others. Sometimes I receive letters like this from the youth with whom I work. Nothing encourages me more, and yet as with so much of life, it is bittersweet. It troubles me that the idea of shadow integration, exploring the inner landscapes of ourselves, is so foreign to our children. We reach a handful of them in high school, a few earlier, but the vast majority aren't guided in these areas at all. Then we're shocked and outraged when violence erupts in the schools, on the streets or at home.

Do you remember a time when you were cut off from the vitality of your youth? Have you had the feeling of having as much energy as the hot sun shining down upon you, then having some cultural or familial rule cap off that sun, that dangerous power, shun it, shame it and throw it away? Has it ever been so painful that your only wish was for a quick death? Not everyone knows this feeling, but many of us do. This is what can happen when these potencies in our youth are driven into shadow. Betrayal in youth is inevitable, it is part of the passage. But nowadays we don't bring the children through. We cut them off at the knees and leave them to lean on the crutches of consumerism.

I have witnessed young people being raised up in their beauty and their blossoming power. There is a quality of surety present, like the ink of a writer's pen touched to clean white paper: no hesitation, no doubt, pure expression. I long for more opportunities like the youth panel on peace I sat with not too long ago. Something glorious happens when the older folks allow themselves to be taught by youth, to be reminded of the complete optimism with which they once were filled. This is some of what I dream for.

If only we could develop a greater appreciation for our rich shadowy interiors—all the marginalized voices in our bodies, cut out because we don't like them—what fine illumination would come forth to guide our destinies. Underneath all of the characters and competing desires lives a pure energy that can neither be created or destroyed. We can reach a place where the presence of a whole and examined awareness becomes real to us, a place where support, learning and expression is available to us. It is clear that a central part of human essence is to share in the light and dark aspects of past, present and even future outcomes. I am encouraged to observe many elders stepping forward at this time and helping us remember to engage in life fully, to take hold, let go, take risks, be in the mix of humanity and the planet unfolding.

This is a process some say we've been at for four million years. Nothing is new here. But like the poet William Stafford suggests, we need reminders lest we fall asleep and lose the thread of our dreams. It is easy enough to stray, to get lazy, to forget our duty, to go numb and shut down. Perhaps it is more difficult than ever to maintain our focus on spiritual matters. In a slow progression that has accelerated drastically in the last hundred years, humans have gained more and more sophisticated tools for altering their physical reality. The ability to grow and harvest food, to have comfortable shelters with reliable heat, water, sewage disposal, has provided us with unprecedented comfort. Perhaps it is human nature to ease up in the midst of such comfort, to imagine matters of spirit are in their right place, or why else would we have it so good? Still, something gnaws at us and we cannot ignore it. Outside appearances may be exceptionally good, materially, but inside, the heat in the belly ebbs. This is our dilemma, I believe, as modern people in a world where technology makes many of the simple tasks of daily living automatic—tasks that once inspired awareness through prayer, ritual, ceremony and passages. What many lose in the bargain is that deep feeling, all the way to the marrow, of being in the center of life's movement while at the same time centerless and part of human elemental flowing. So how do we gain back that edge, that strong feeling of wellness that defines one's gifts, a kind of body aliveness that comes from struggling for survival, when it appears, on the surface, that we have it made?

I don't believe the answer is necessarily easy or, on the contrary, impossibly difficult. Each of us has our own code of human nature. It is never the same code twice. The place to start is with the heart. It will tell you in no uncertain terms if you are living in a way that fulfills heart matters. If the heart is quiet, refuses to inform you because of too many lonely years, and has atrophied, yet you are ready to leap anyway, someone might catch you. There are no guarantees, and still it is a risk worth taking.

Teachings and experiences in nature, like extreme solitude that opens us to new arenas of consciousness (sometimes called transformative events), are often not easy experiences, or friendly, but are still necessary. Their power, however, doesn't come fully alive unless we return and lay it in a field of friendship. Otherwise, the epiphany we may have glimpsed can quickly get tucked into the carpetbag. True friendship is like a light spring rain that encourages the tiny shoots of growth to green up, and take on the task of coming to fruit. These friends, these soul mates, are the nutrition that keeps the transformative experiences alive and believable. Churches, schools, neighborhoods and places of work, may include these kinds of friendships. Asking for support is a courageous action, and one that ought to be admired and encouraged, not only for the adult population but especially for the youth. It is a truism to say that life is too much for any one of us to carry alone, and yet our culture often looks askance at those who ask for help. It seems to me that when one speaks of human nature one can also conclude that asking for support, calling for help or healing, is as natural and normal and necessary as the sunrise in the morning.

It is human to be unable to see oneself, to need the reflection of caring others. Jung and the whole Jungian school came to the awareness of shadow forces in the study of dreams and various forms of consciousness other than normal waking awareness. They learned that shadow forms do not voluntarily come into the light for acceptance and integration. They need to be invited, encouraged, and worked with in creative ways by those who can listen to and mirror and flesh out their substance. This is the way of nature as well, to hold us in the silence so that we may see unknown truths about ourselves. People have gone into solitude with nature for the type of reflection available in therapy or group processes. More will be said about nature and solitude in a later chapter. For now, the important message the elders speak of is to listen inside, truly pay attention to the whole body truth, the heart voice. If things aren't working, seek the reflection of those with experience in such matters, and also let time in nature help in the opening up and seeing of a fuller, more substantive quality of being.

I've been in my men's lodge and numerous other circles during the last fifteen years, and have witnessed this process many times. There is something mysterious and wonderful that occurs when men are able to reconstitute old wounds and unappreciated aspects of themselves into current time. It is nothing short of rebirth—like Nelson Mandella locked in a cell for twenty years, a treasure, put there because he was a threat to the status quo. This is what the mind does in our personal soul apartheid to the dangerous voices inside of us, the rebel leader who envisions a different way. We lock away unimaginable genius, all the while putting forth propaganda—mostly to ourselves—about how wicked and subversive the prisoner is, and how we really have no choice and must keep him locked away. But as we have seen with the release of Nelson Mandella, there is beauty and power in the prisoner. By freeing and integrating our own factional leaders, we too have the potential of bringing forth a new era in our own lives, a rebirth, a renaissance. I have had the pleasure of watching such rebirths take place when lost parts of men are brought back, freed from their shackles and from the hatred that holds them in the penitentiary. It is miraculous. The change may originate in the psyche, but it goes to a cellular level. The soul strengthening takes place in very tangible, physical ways. There is no mistaking it when this transformational energy shows up. Certain rituals bring it forth. Prayers of one kind or another, spoken a certain way or at a certain time with a degree of sincerity, draw out the unconscious powers. Sometimes metaphorical plays in which other people play roles from our lives can unlock the prison gates. So many ways, such mystery and beauty.

One time in particular, at a retreat in Colorado, a man came forward with the story of a life way, a certain attitude, that had been with him a long time and no longer served him. He expressed a feeling of dampening, loss of passion, a lack of zest or even desire to continue living. With the help of his own imagination and desire, he called on the community and the elders to bring the story out of his body so he could wrestle with it. He crafted, with the help of us all, a way to bring out the voices that were contributing to his loss of heart and passion. The work took the form of ritual theater, in which many of the men played the parts of these inner voices. At one point the man was covered by a blanket of his own making, terrified to be held down, crying out for help and the reclaiming of his heart. The men around the circle understood this kind of suffering. They held each other and wept as he fought his epic battle. Eventually the man fought from under the blanket and took back his heart from the character he perceived as holding it. It was one of those moments of triumph, when ritual is every bit as real as day-to-day experience, and stands as an example of the power in wrestling with and reclaiming the lost parts of ourselves.

Men have taught me this at spirit camps and gatherings, dances, sweats, in letters and simple conversations over coffee. They have shown through their own courageous struggles how true it is that our projections thrown onto the world only serve us if we take them back and appreciate them not as objective truths, but some manifestation of an inner dynamic. This to me is the cusp of what might be called human evolution. When we realize that eighty or ninety percent of what we perceive has little if any relationship to what is actually going on, we are naturally less arrogant, self-righteous or aggressive. Quantum physics, in its study of energy and matter, tells us everything is a paradox (energetically). Nothing can be contained by rules or someone's opinion of it. The men I have known who begin to work with these ideas become quite different than they were before. It's almost as if they become another species, carrying some of the qualities of their former selves, but alive to a whole new world. They become willing, even grateful, to give up positions, certainties, attitudes that seemed central to their characters because it becomes clear they no longer serve them or their community.

We have met in lodges and Boy Scout camps, some with hot water, others without, and have cooked our own meals. We have met in wood lots surrounded by farmer's fields, in deserts and high mountain valleys with tents and tarps for shelters. And we have met in classy conference centers with fully catered meals. We've been frozen by stinging rain and hail, baked crisp by the sun without a cloud for days, eaten alive by various biting insects, washed out by flash floods, and also had many beautiful gentle days next to calm lakes, quiet streams, tranquil sage brush and stoic mountain peaks. In each case, it has been a privilege to be in a circle of men, to join with them in the inquiry of the great mystery. When the weather has turned and given us a new set of conditions to deal with, we have gained new gifts by being shaped in the strong hands of nature.

One time, at my colleague Joe Laur's place in northern Minnesota, it began to rain, and I mean sheets of it for days. After the third day, the trails around camp turned into mud troughs three and four inches deep. We slogged around in the muck, drenched, limited, powerless to make it different. To say that nature brought us to our shadows is an understatement. What could we do? Sit around and bitch about it? We could do that, but that wasn't our purpose for gathering, so we cursed for awhile, then danced our anger, our disappointment, our murky voices, felt the cold, the agitation. We noticed how the chill settled into our joints and reminded us of our aging, the passages we were in and the difficulties we faced even in our homes where rain and cold could not touch us.

Joseph Jastrab,[27] a wilderness guide and soul-working man from the northeast states, handled the rain by packing us into a tiny log cabin with no windows. We would sit in there and sing and counsel and get pushed around by our own discomfort until we simply had to break out of that cauldron of humanity and move on. The soul wishes so much for us to be the whole being we are. This endurance of weather was another way to learn about the unconscious, hidden and waiting to emerge, waiting for the right time, the circumstance when our armor would drop and something could get through to us. Blessed be.

Another man with a flute, a wild Canadian artist named Toque, played his music and guided us to our depths with the help of the winds, birds, poplar and balsam. His music softened our psyches and the mental grip the mind often keeps on the less strident voices inside of ourselves. This calls for emphasis: music, rhythm, song, are powerful vehicles for opening us to deeper ways of understanding. Music alters our usual mode of perception and allows us to drop away some of the habitual filters and hear in new ways, hear *ourselves* as we are in the present. And so music, like prayer, works as a key that opens gateways of perception otherwise closed to us. Music is often the element that opens the ritual to spirit realms and counsel communication to the heart. Toque's flute music allowed us to embrace our stories and receive the blessings of them being shared, passed along and sent back with appreciation.

After each day of learning how to stay mostly dry, singing, getting frustrated in a pig's paradise of mud, engaging rituals, offering prayers — some planned, others bursting forth from a man's guts with the force of a bear rumbling out of the woods—we paused to give thanks. So much beauty rose out of this muck. There could be no denying the power of ritual wrapped in prayer to bring deep healing, regardless of what dumped from the skies. At this and other gatherings, I've witnessed profound shifts in mens' understandings of who they are and what they're moving toward. Men who have been victims and perpetrators of generational sexual abuse have stopped it and begun the healing, *not just of themselves*, but of their ancestors. Hidden grief and pain so heavy on their souls it literally hurt to move was lifted up, embraced, invited out to be seen, dialogued with, cared for and released to the sky or the depths of the earth. Let us remember how much practice and natural skill the earth has at processing grief, pain, hatred, rage. Left inside of ourselves, these energies clog, suffocate, rupture and hemorrhage, stifle, fester and leave us ill. The earth, yes, the earth can break them down. These voices—any of them, even those ready for the compost pile—can be made into something that fuels the soul. In this way they are not discarded, but reworked by the forces of nature in the emerging self.

I have heard that some First Nation people learn early on to go out alone, dig a hole, and scream their hatreds, their furies, their pain, loss, bitterness, into the hole, and the earth will generously accept it. The earth knows what to do with these things when we do not.

I've watched men entrenched in conflicts so old they seem to have been around longer than they have. And these men have claimed their part, the ways they have done damage, and committed themselves to making amends. Men who have raped, been the victims of rape, men who have killed, whose own souls have been murdered, each of them, in countless unique and fascinating ways, breaking through—with the help of their ancestors—to new possibilities. Men have pulled their guts out, like dressing a deer, to work openly with the struggles that have been eating them up from the inside out. They've pulled up childhood wounds, cultural shame, their violence, numbing hatred and stood in the fire of their now naked passion and said, *This is my life! I want it back!* They meet their yearning, newly emancipated, hungry, furious, stunned, unbearably sad, and hear it proclaim—undaunted by anything that has happened—the right of every man, woman and child to live and know beauty, richness, peace and joy, to wander in the great mystery with dignity. Their yearning for love meets them on the field of acceptance.

Every once in awhile during that one rainy encampment, Joe Laur would pull us to the fire pit. The young men tended the fire. The elders stayed close for warmth. Joe began to tell jokes. He poked fun at himself and at us, and the laughter—whew!—what a blessing. I have heard it said by a Central American shaman that if a ritual, no matter how serious, does not contain humor and is incapable of laughing at itself, it is incomplete, and will often sabotage itself. I've found this to be true time and time again. Whenever we start getting inflated, imagine ourselves in some rarefied strata unavailable to the common man, inevitably something foolish comes in and changes the whole direction. I'm not suggesting that we inject some sort of irreverence into prayer. I've seen humor break tension or piss somebody off, reminding us that ritual can be held too tightly, that we can take ourselves too seriously. What is important is to remain open to different worlds, the physical world and the spirit world. Sometimes the irreverence itself can jolt us back into awareness.

These are the little joys, like Joe's jokes around the fire at that soggy gathering, that keep us strong and sustain our faith. I don't think it would be possible to venture among inner shadow lands rife with danger if we didn't know that something humorous flits through the miasma like a court jester firefly, and with its tiny flickering light, helps us locate the nuggets of gold. Chogyam Trungpa, a Tibetan lama, said in 1978:

> Sense of humor does not necessarily mean laughing at jokes. Jokes are quite different from a sense of humor. Sense of humor means being able to see clearly and being able to see through things. You begin to appreciate the workings of your mind and the workings of the situations that are given to you. You have some sense of natural celebration. You have a sense of healthiness and togetherness. You have a sense of openness and possibilities. You have settled into your world and are not threatened by possibilities of other worlds. You can perform your activities so freely, so well, so beautifully. There is a kind of tidiness throughout your whole life.

It was a tradition of sorts, at these gatherings in the boreal forests of northern Minnesota, that John Lee[28] would step in, aclaimed author, poet and soul healing guide, and call the focus back in before we were all carried off by the fool and missed the dance entirely. John would take poems of his own, and others, and help us find our way back into the core of remembering the reasons we came, remembering the prayers of the poets that focus and gather us.

These times over the years, with much laughter and prayers, in the esteemed company of elders (both human and geologic), have inspired men to find themselves, their voices and their places in the world. Those who plunged in despite their skepticism, learned something of their inner terrain and the longing that motivates them. They became rich with their own spirits and souls set free to speak, move, sweat, dance, laugh, cry and hold with compassion the truth of their lives. They have recognized an inherited soul biology that dates us back more than three million years. The best stories are the ones that have been told a thousand times, renewed on each occasion by the fresh life that tells it. Could this be our destiny, as the Norse pathfinder says, to keep the thread connected? Are we part of an invisible web of soul, and in some way asked to tend it, to mend a broken strand, and to reinforce the edges by our own spidery silk of commitment and responsibility?

In Michael Gurian's book, *The Good Son*,[29] he speaks of the male biology, the inheritance, if you will, being several million years old. He says, and current brain research backs this up, that men are spatially oriented, an evolution that serves our obligations to the people to provide meat and protection. We are less social, less receptive to certain qualities such as nurturing. These are the qualities that served us during long periods of solitude on the hunt, or protracted battles with relentless enemies. With this biological, blood and tissue component to our souls, we have an essence or substrate that influences everything we do. It comes as no surprise that men in general aren't drawn to explorations of shadow and the deep feeling work that seems so important. Becoming too engrossed in one's feelings might lead to a slight sluggishness in the field, and cost a man his life. I find this an extremely interesting possibility. It explains much of what I have experienced in my work.

We also come from a tribal heritage where men lived in communities of brothers and large family circles. The nuclear family is a new concept that is, as far as I can tell, threatening to men. There is something confining about it. It seems to require more of an individual—be it father or mother—than is natural for us. If the demands resting on one man's shoulders weigh too heavily on his heart, he often falls apart, and his soul becomes hungry. Some of this is evidenced by so many men abandoning their families, so many single mothers. For men to be able to work in nuclear family units, to have the degree of contact with spouses and children now being asked of them, new behaviors have to be learned. A new manhood is asked of us. Part of the new model involves men going into the unconscious realms, the wounds, the historical shadows, places they are not comfortable with, or that do not feel natural to us. These are the introspective places we have been speaking of: self-generated and cultural projections, the emotions, wounds, the anima, where compassion and empathy can be cultivated. It no longer works for men to simply click onto the cultural icon of commercial dictates. I have been shown the value of doing soul work by hundreds of men from the full range of backgrounds and socioeconomic status. What awaits us in the evolving model of manhood is not an amputation or disfiguring of our natures. Rather, an enriching and deepening, a spiritual home, painted with meaning, laid with the bricks of value, purpose, destiny. We are trapped and tricked into thinking we can find this place, or build this soul house, what David Whyte calls "The House of Belonging," with money, glitzy toys, "trophy" women. I'm hearing men call for a reversal of this cultural shadow, at least a naming of it and acknowledgment of its power, its status as a false truth, backed up by a million dollar ad campaign. We live at a time of transition and the current myth doesn't empower us to tackle it. What is being asked, to my way of thinking, is a turn toward the inner life, and an honest assessment of the forces that drive us crazy when we can no longer sustain our faith in the god of money.

Is the mastery of this way of living the actual goal? For many of us it is not. It is more a remembering that teaches us and informs us. If these inward journeys are leaned into enough we begin to know, in our own bodies, our own truths. One of them, that comes up again and again, is that we do belong in this life, and we *are* charged with the great wisdom of Spirit. We *do* have the necessary task of showing up and contributing to human evolution.

ONE OF MY DESIRES IN TELLING THESE STORIES IS TO EXPAND WHAT we consider prayer, the ways in which it is practiced, its forms and its possibilities. My experience of prayer, its efficacy and power, shows that there are countless ways into the beauty of prayer. Rather than place dogma and preference around the potential of prayer, I look for ways to integrate and blend, to find the union between the sacred and the profane. I have never seen prayer limited by where it was taking place, what language it was said in, what garb was being worn, what book was being referenced. In a similar way, solitude, or simply being alone, can be experienced as an expanded horizon so that we can enjoy its benefits more often, be fed from it more regularly, regardless of where we live or what we do.

I remember standing in a phone booth in downtown Toronto, surrounded by thick clouds of noise, exhaust, bustling people, speeding cars and trucks. There I was in a lonely moment, faced with some difficult news and caught in the rush of people and machines, when I felt moved to pray, right there in the phone booth, in the middle of the chaos. I asked for guidance and support, and opened myself to whatever might be there for me. I did not have to dial zero for the operator. In those few short moments in a glass enclosure, I found solitude, and walked out of the phone booth surprised to find my dilemma lighter and my awareness more acute. I could suddenly see that my struggle existed in *that moment*, and that the best I can do is be present, and come into myself right there in the city.

I am reminded now of the four universal practices of awakening revealed by Angeles Ariens[30] in her exploration of spiritual traditions around the world. The first practice is to show up. Simple. Show up.

Wherever, whenever…show up. The second practice is to pay attention. Show up and pay attention. Third, be honest. Speak your personal truth from your heart, without judgment or blame. Finally, be unattached to outcome. Do not imagine you can control the results but leave that with faith. In these ways, we can make ourselves available to the moments of solitude that are present in our lives.

Returning to the occasion in the phone booth in Toronto, I saw after a few moments of solitude and prayer that I could not control my dilemma. All I could do was be as present as possible to my current reality, to my thoughts and feelings and what happened around me. It is somewhat ironic that I found solitude in such a crowded, noisy place. It made clear to me that solitude is not predicated on geographical space. It is the practice of going inside the body, finding separation and aloneness from that which may distract. This allows the sorting out of confusion and gives voice to the soul, which speaks to us in subtle ways beyond the force of logic to interpret.

There is something profoundly important about this separation into solitude as a part of spiritual awakening throughout the ages. So many forms have included solo time: quiet, separate from others, with inner listening. It seems valuable that each of us define what this means to us, and devise ways to reach the place on a regular basis. To me, solitude is any time or gathering of moments when I can take an account of my internal condition, can listen to my body wisdom, my embodiment. Solitude is a time when one pays attention to the energies and voices inside. I can sense my body suspended in a web of life, and yet separate unto itself, its own heart beating, lungs filling and emptying. It's not about disconnecting from the pulse of the earth, but connecting with the wonder in that moment where the mind aligns itself with the wonder: the elemental, biological soul of true intelligence we all share and have equal access to. In solitude we remember to remember the encoded wisdom of the million plus years experience that runs through each cell of our bodies. Meaning, the ballast of soul-weighted living, thrives on solitude. We can each replenish our ballast of meaning in the simple practice of vital solitude. In so doing, we contribute to the timeless ancestral pools that are filled by our drinking from them. Our solitude is the offering of our lives into the greater weave, our contribution, a strand of gold and crimson, that contributes to the evolution of humankind.

The action of taking solitude and bearing witness to the natural world around and through us is a prayerful condition. One of the central themes of prayer as I have witnessed and practiced is the quality of true listening. This quality goes beyond merely hearing. It goes beyond the cognitive skill of understanding a message and formulating a reply. True listening is that hearing that almost transcends the listener, that leaves him mute, open and deeply touched. Certain music has this affect, and almost all of us have been touched by music. I would propose that we can listen to each other as if each of us speaks a symphony or the melody of an Indian flute. So too, our own hearts play ballads of immense beauty and wonder when we find the time, take the solitude, and listen. Louise Gopfert-March has said this about the process:

> The first step is learning to hear, wanting to hear, releasing the chaos within oneself, releasing it in the way one releases the body in physical death. This step means that one no longer wants to interfere, to change things,…to quarrel, to express an opinion, to translate what was heard into everyday mechanical language…[It] means that one rests easy next to the giant army of onrushing thoughts, feelings and physical things. The ability to hear is a difficult thing.[31]

This surrender, letting go as if life itself were being shed, has far reaching implications. It strikes me as such an ancient and practical attitude to cultivate. Life has always been difficult and stressful. Our modern times do not have a monopoly on such things. What we do have now, in my judgment, is a shortage of means by which to relieve our stress, to dissipate the will that seeks control and power against the difficult forces of life. We glorify a "work hard/play hard" ideal that often neglects the essential replenishing that comes from bathing in the mysterious waters of detached solitude. It has been said in the meditative traditions, particularly tai chi, that to be able to relax is the paramount ability in developing one's art, and delivering oneself to the world. The easing of constraints in the body, in the thoughts, letting go of striving, objective goals, all the judgments and attitudes of living in the chaos of society, allows the experience of deeper meaning. To touch the unknown and surrender one's will, one's mind and even emotions, allows an altered and enriching form of being to come forth.

One of the most profound and accessible ways to engage in this nourishing surrender is to go into nature. To let go into the body and touch one's own nature and the natural world is to be released into a container that can hold heart and soul safely, and is, in fact, designed to do so. These times of grace in nature can help us realize that the beauty of humanity and the beauty of all life are inseparable. Without the benefit of time in nature, a dangerous separation can harm the soul. It seems important that we remember where we come from, that for millions of years we have been fortified and nourished by an almost continual bathing in wild natural waters. The natural world and all the elements of life run through our souls as they did through our ancestors. When we step into times of solitude in nature, we are stepping into ourselves, and in so doing, we find our inner unity held by the outer unity. This unity is present to us anywhere, as stated earlier, in an expanded definition of solitude. Nonetheless, time in nature seems to invite the gifts of solitude more readily than other environments.

Modern man has difficulty understanding this. So much of what we have created seems to conspire against solitude and time in nature. We have created a society in which our own constructions, our technologies and forms of commerce, have become so demanding they have literally consumed us. Few of us have any "free" time and we have had little choice but to convince ourselves this is a glorious thing and proof of our importance. The soul being, however, isn't happy. What it knows and where it comes from, in accord with indigenous ways, was when people spent something like fifty to eighty percent of their time in nature, in ritual and soulful practices. Much of the remaining time was spent in the wild—hunting, gathering food, bathing in the stream— essentially embracing our holy chores. Our bodies are hard-wired to expect a life rhythm like this—as was practiced for the vast majority of our existence. In our bones, as much as we know we need food, water and air, we know also how essential are prayer and ritual. Yet today we have managed to turn it around so that we work fifty to eighty percent of the time, and are so tired from it the most appealing form of leisure is often the passive receiving of entertainment from television, movies or sporting events. This is not wrong. No one is to blame. The patriarchy didn't do it. The church didn't do it. We all did it. We're all in it together, and responsible for our own soul survival. If there is the potential of a better way, we choose it together and begin living it today. It is tiring and draining to be bothered by what is wrong in the world. It draws off our vitality to sit around with friends and complain about everything that is wrong in the world. Instead, more and more men are choosing a simple life. Seeing the beauty of simplicity, and making life a statement that envisions what it can be. "Be the change you want to see in the world," said Joseph Chilton Pearce, quoting Mahatma Gandhi. To sit around and complain about everything that is wrong is in many ways a form of acceptance. It puts it out there as the fault of *them*, and nothing can be done about it. This perspective is not working.

In 1993, I went with three other men into the hills of northeast Utah to fast and pray. One of the men was having a difficult time with his pack on the way into base camp. The thick willow bushes growing along the small spring next to the path tangled and thrashed him. He grumbled and fought and it was clear he carried for us modern man's resentment toward life when it doesn't go his way. Nothing we could do as fellow travelers could help him. I smiled and thanked the willows for helping the man see himself, and showing us our entanglements with our own will.

On his solo, he went up the canyon wall and perched himself on a rock shelf that was at the entrance of a deep red rock fissure. He played his flute and the music dissipated his striving into the surrounding red sandstone. Breathing with the concentration of his music, he took in the pungent aroma of sage brush, observed the acrobatic swallows darting through the air, heard their call, and began to fill with the generosity of solitude and the air of mystery. By the time he returned to base camp several days later, it was difficult to imagine him the same man who had grumbled and complained the whole way in. It seemed as if some great burden had been lifted from him. His bitterness about the way his life had gone, or the way the world had received him, took a new shape, one he could work with and be renewed by. Instead of bitterness and helplessness, he glowed with a genuine compassion and a healthy grief that was the beginning of his healing. I could see it in the color of his face. He was now a part of it, a man of caring and kindness for people and the beauty of the earth. This is what he taught us: to remember ourselves and to live by the lesson.

I don't have any illusions that this one experience in nature healed this man completely. More than likely, he went back to his life in the city and fell into the same struggles with which he came. I do know that his time in nature brought him into an ancient wisdom, and for that time he was not a loose gear spinning in emptiness. Perhaps he developed a practice out of that seed time. I can only hope so. The soul, it seems, is not impressed with big cathartic events. It likes little daily bits of nourishment. It likes to hear the conscious mind return to the nugget of wisdom, again and again, in the same manner a baby returns to the breast over and over again and never tires of the milk.

I have been a part of prayers in nature with men for many years, in mountains and deserts and lake shores, each time guiding them to solitude. The guide does not make it happen. My job, like that of a midwife, is to hold a container: a conscious place made strong with my own preparation, prayer and commitment. Anything else that happens is up to the individual and the voices in nature. Sometimes it doesn't appear to work for people and they may become disappointed. I wish this were never the case, and yet the work requires each of us to answer the call of mystery and participation in human evolution in our own ways. When men take solo time in nature, most often they return with a changed anatomy—their cells vibrating at a different frequency, renewed in their feeling of purpose and meaning. I have witnessed these transformations so many times, and need no convincing of the power such practice holds. The bravery of the men, their courage and willingness to go out into it alone, brings me joy and appreciation for the essential human character. When men go out alone, undisturbed by phone calls, e-mail, deadlines and the banal practicalities of a civilized society, they meet their true natures and they come back with a joy that lies on them as a fine garment, visible all over their bodies. They literally find lost parts of themselves and life truths that allow them to be in their grounded nature and thus enriched for the journey through life's mysteries—challenges and pain, as well as joys, victories and pleasures.

Something about solitude brings about a disarming of the usual defenses we carry around to protect ourselves. Whether it's a Manhattan apartment or a cornfield in Iowa, the ability to receive solitude, to fall into the witnessing place, allows the opening to occur. Without contact in this place of opening, men seem to lose contact with their true selves. This feeling of separation troubles them, often in ways they can't quite grasp, but shows up in outbursts of rage, depression, worry and aggressive behavior that threatens the well being of the community. As aware, mature men, these sensations of discomfort (being bothered, melancholy for no apparent reason) provide us clues that our inner world needs tending. These are the times to ask ourselves, as the medicine man advised, "What blocks me? What keeps me from the wisdom of heart and soul?" In this way, we take back our projections. We stop seeing a "problem" out there that vexes us, and look to the source of our feelings which always resides within us. If I am irritated, perhaps rather than go after someone or something that appears to be the cause, it is best to seek solitude and listen with the ears of my heart to my inner voices, to my body. In this practice, men can stay grounded. The body comes back to life. That which imagined itself unwelcome, forever banished and unwanted in the prison of some internal organ, can come forward and be held and witnessed in its beauty. From this generative and receptive state comes a way of being.

When a man, or any adult, goes into solitude and prayer, according to his own timing and method, and lets go of the chaos of everyday life, he brings back to his community, family, and himself, information that helps them find ground, direction and a home for soul. I've seen men at the retreats I guide go out and sit by a pond, or walk three miles through thick boreal forest, or take a nap, or watch hummingbirds play in a clearing, or inspect the bugs crawling around the bottom of a creek. Some sing, some weep, wail, pound on the earth, smash dead trees with rotting logs, and a thousand other things. They return (it rarely fails) informed by the experience, by the nuance of nature, their dreams and meditations, and find their spiritual direction altered for the remainder of the retreat. Sometimes, this course correction shifts a man's life completely. Whatever the results of these times in solitude, there is no question they feed the soul. What does it take for us to give this gift to ourselves on a regular basis? How do we re-learn or remember the fundamental need for solitude in our lives?

We have become a society that is possessed with short-term vision and the false sense that to have the comfort of material things is the way home, the way to inner peace. None of the men I have ever worked with found peace through external means. I cannot remember any of my elders or spiritual teachers who spoke to me about finding my heart and soul home by seeking material comfort. And yet, paradoxically, many of us, most of us, possibly, must travel this path some distance before we discover its shortcomings. The Information Age supplies ample teaching in this regard. The speed and pressure of accelerated expectations, being busy and consuming ever more products does not satisfy the ancient desire to be at home with who we are in meaning and purpose. More often than not it creates frustration and anger.

I have yet to meet a man who can avoid the normal, natural yearning toward a life of meaning and a part in human evolution. Unfortunately, it appears our society conspires in ever more devious ways to push us further away from the soul quenching times of solitude and introspection. We live in a time of decline and cultural fracturing. Our social institutions are breaking down. Family, community, religion, trust in spirit and prayer, trust in ourselves even, are all faltering. Through our hands slips the ancient wisdom all the gods have entrusted in our care. We seem to be crumbling into a pile of compost, and from it may come an eventual remembering, a sprout of insight that will lead us back to kindness and compassion, the cessation of war against ourselves and our fellow humans throughout the world. Solitude will once again become an important ingredient in the course of human evolution.

Our modern culture sets up a contradiction between genuine and artificial yearnings. We can't help but engage in the natural decomposing, and yet we deceive ourselves through a compelling mythology that tells us we are ascending, rising to a godliness through our mastery of nature. It is a mythology of technology, powerful and dominating. Like a Russian thistle imported to warmer climates, the myth of progress chokes out all other views. More and more deeply sheltered in our possessions and technologies, it is difficult if not impossible to recognize the lost horizon of solitude, meaning and purpose.

I remember one of my early lessons in solitude and the severe elements of nature. It came on my first ice fishing trip with my Grampa, Louis Engle, on Lake Erie. We got going at what was an absurdly early hour for a boy, having left home before my daily rendezvous with Jungle Jim at 6:30 on channel four. Before the sun had risen, we walked in the freezing wind a mile out onto the ice. Grampa pulled a wooden sled, loaded with our fishing gear, some food and a thermos of hot cocoa. He said nothing to me. There was only the sound of wind, the crunch of our boots on the ice, the scratch of the wooden sled and an expanse of white that stretched forever.

I could feel myself walking into the longest day of my life.

Grampa appeared impervious to the harsh conditions. He carried himself with the radiant loneliness of a wild orchid, somehow thriving in those frigid conditions. I knew him mostly by watching him work at the simple tasks of a fine craftsman. He was a lineman (for the county), but his skills covered all the trades. He carved his own bird decoys, did house wiring, carpentry, welding. I can remember watching him work on old pipes with a pot of melted lead pouring out toxic fumes while he ladled it out to seal joints. He could work on anything. His words to me, when they came, were something like, "Slow down and watch this. You may need to know this yourself someday." Watching him was like watching an artist create. The pace was always slow, punctuated by long pauses while he thought out what to do next. Whether he was picking tomato worms off his seven-foot plants or preparing for a three-week hunting trip to Colorado, he operated in that calculated silence.

It was this quiet powerful man I followed onto the ice that morning in search of perch. Eventually he stopped, without warning, and began to spud out a ten-inch hole in the deep ice with a heavy steel rod.

In his deliberate way, he opened five holes, baited the tip-ups (handmade ice fishing poles), and unfolded the canvas seats on which we would wait for signs of action. Grampa would watch three holes. I had two.

Now and then the vast ice made a deep long groan, broken by loud bone cracking sounds. It was like a thunder at times, or the explosion of a high powered rifle, the crack starting somewhere in the distance, moving through us and then carrying miles out into the lake. I thought we might get swallowed up. You always heard about somebody falling through. Grampa didn't seem to notice. He was like the archetypal hunter who had determined emotions lack utility.

Eventually I relaxed and concentrated on my two holes in the ice. I had to keep the water moving or the ice would quickly close them off. Inside of myself, the ice also began to form. Cold turned to pain, concentration into a sort of shamanic trance. I stared into those dark holes, too cold even to shiver, and in some way went down in there with the fish, down into the bottom where who I thought I was no longer existed. Every so often I came back up and looked at Grampa, sitting there with no gloves on his thick red hands. He became for me an Eskimo spirit, half real and half god. It amazed me that I was in so much pain, while Grampa appeared to be in harmonious meditation with the ice, the wind and the cold. His silent presence augmented my solitude, threw me deeper into the questions of potency that begin to trouble a boy of ten or eleven. Did I have what it takes to be a man? Would I be able to have sex? Hold a job and survive on my own?

Mercifully, the day finally ended. It seems we caught fish, though I have no recollection of it. We rode home with our buckets of perch in Grampa's '63 VW bug. When we got to his place, Gram warmed me up with her award-winning noodle soup, a handful of her old-world Lebkucken cookies, and the warmest, jolliest heart a grandson could ask for. The three of us cleaned the fish and packed them in white paper for gifts and future suppers.

This experience sticks with me thirty-seven years later. I can still see clearly the form of the old man sitting silently on the ice, a holy monk, wordless and waiting. This image walks with me into my work. I often wish I could surprise all of the men one day, come to their places of work, and convince them to go out with me onto Grampa's ice.

Essentially, we do something similar at our gatherings. Removal from the familiar comforts opens a hole in the ice around the soul. Much of what gets pulled up from the unconscious stream has to do with the painful discovery of an unsatisfying life lived out of a lie. The cultural promise of purchased contentment is seen for the sham that it is. When men feel in their bodies the disconnection of the current social norm, the outburst of feeling can be terrifying. The break from a frozen numbness of spiritual isolation is often explosive.

I remember the time in an alpine meadow near Estes Park, Colorado, when an elder became angry about some of the ways the camp was evolving. He expressed his displeasure and confronted a number of men—including those of us who were the guides. After the elder spoke his mind we sat in silence, discharged, our minds laid to rest in the sunshine and the soft breeze through the aspen. The cleansed stillness became a gateway for a young man to take the lid off of a suppressed way of living that had troubled him for years. (And we thought the fireworks were over!) Because an elder had expressed his anger, this young man could let his authentic nature come forth. Every rock and tree and blue gold columbine cried out for him to let his true being emerge. I had known this man for years. He is a great and honorable bow hunter, a man of prayer who feels most alive out in the wilderness.

In that moment, with nearly thirty men having just been washed with the clear anger of the camp elder, the young man erupted. His focal point became the watch on his right wrist, such a fixture in his life the skin underneath was pale white with the outline of the time piece. He tore it off and began pounding on it with a big hunk of ponderosa pine. He screamed at it as a symbol of his contained nature, its force as a reminder of what he didn't have time to do, the demands and pressures of a life that never leaves him time for the simple joys of the heart. The watch itself had power over him. Like so many of us the clock or the daytimer, the pager, the cell phone, has become the dictator.

To call the scene dramatic wouldn't begin to describe this drama played out in the immense theater of granite cliffs, cobalt blue skies, the screech of red tailed hawks, the croak of ravens, the gurgle of the creek, and the spellbound wonder of witnessing and being witnessed in the vastness of nature. The young man's fury didn't last more than five minutes, but the story it told goes all the way back to the first pressures of domestication, the demands of planting and harvesting that deprived us of a hunter-gatherer's freedom. All of us knew the story, our own versions of it, the ways in which punching time clocks and meeting deadlines had confused many of our lives. What the young man did there he did for probably all the men in camp. It was ritual in the most complete sense, representing a healing for the whole community, no matter how personal it appeared.

At other times, the expressions of discontent can be quiet and unassuming, a quiet melting away of armor that reveals a soft, sad, beautiful despair. I remember the gentle man with long red hair who wept in my arms most of a foggy evening under the soft patter of a steady mountain rain. He was sad, for so many reasons, and as we joined him in his grief, our many sadnesses came out. The soft rain and steady dripping from the trees told us nature understood.

Sometimes hysterical, maniacal laughter bursts forth, like the time we were sitting in a lodge and some spark got a couple of us laughing. There seemed to be a large store of fuel there, waiting to be ignited. Suddenly everything we were doing became absurd, and the seriousness we put on it made it even more absurd. We couldn't stop laughing. The fool had come to dance. He reminded us that even the most important ritual has a comic element to it. The comedy wants to be honored equally with the reverence.

When the container, the ritual space, is defined, remembered and respectful, anything of benefit that wants to come may come. Gravely important here is to ask Spirit to bring in that which is of benefit. A wise teacher of mine pointed that out many years ago. He, being an authentic healer for most of his life, knew there were plenty of spirit energies that are harmful to people and are best avoided. The cathedral of nature, I have found, makes the strongest container. Nature is the original temple, the original church, synagogue, mosque, where we went to be held in our prayers, rituals and inquiries, where we found guidance, understanding, inspiration, the great reflection.

Fifteen years in this work has shown me that when men step away from their civilized, domesticated comforts they find out who they really are and why they have come to this life. It takes a separation from the over-stimulating, high pressure world, and an entry into the place of solitude and prayer, in a sacred brotherhood, to be available to the guidance. Here, men find the right environment to make the basic choice between life and death. They can and do take on a self-directed, self-aware, approach to living. They question and often reject the spoon-fed reality of others, of the dominant culture, prejudiced religions and the mass media.

This is not a new process. People throughout the history of civilization have continually questioned the values of their culture, and gone in new directions. We come to status quo, live in it for awhile, and eventually begin to question it, to see what isn't working and find better ways. We journey inward to see where we have come from and how it is we can better thrive with the heart as the guiding force. Our times are different only because of the sheer scale involved. What we do is impactful in a clearly visible way on the world around us. We have weapons of destruction and forms of energy production that can literally end the life of everything on earth. When we sit down to question the current model of living, the stakes are higher than they have ever been before. It used to be that nature offered the greatest threat to our survival. Ice ages, draught, famine, flood, disease—these used to be our greatest dangers. Now it is us. We ourselves are the greatest danger to our survival.

That we can actually destroy millions of lives in an instant is a responsibility humanity has not yet learned how to hold. Our technologies have evolved much faster than our biology, which changes so very slowly over eons. We try to tell ourselves that we can keep up, that we are like our space ships and are ascending toward god. But something draws us down into the compost. It tells us we cannot go where our technology leads us, that we are earth creatures, that our truth and greatness lies in the simplicity of rock and soil and grass. Here we find our God, and know our oneness.

In Malidoma Somé's book, *Of Water and the Spirit,*[32] he speaks about how his elders from the Dagara people of West Africa helped him know, that "remembering means submitting to your fate." From this place of remembering he was able to receive the spiritual support and guidance of his ancestors. He was able to know in his body awareness when his living was full and rich with meaning and purpose. His elders helped him see that "being sick memory" (forgetting his soul purpose) is often the cause for life's paralyzing struggles.

What we are talking about in this chapter and other parts of the book truly becomes clear through the concepts of solitude, nature and prayer. Prayer, as I have witnessed it, has a tendency to soften the membrane of the psyche and allow the entry of non-ordinary information. Prayer also softens the cellular shells in the most primary way throughout the body. Thus the whole body spectrum is penetrated and brought into awareness, the intelligence of receptor and sender. Prayer helps men be permeated, in the deepest, most primary way, by the true purpose of their lives. Solitude, whether in nature or at home, inside or at a park, is the time for refining the energy served up to the listener by prayer and remembering. I have seen this wisdom transmitted to countless men, and the women and youth with whom I have worked. The healing and vision of a remembered destiny, of a life truly inspired and infused with meaning, comes to people in times of solitude, especially in nature. Nature is an elemental form, as is humanity, that contains within itself the diversity and mixture of the four basic elements of life: Earth (the west, adulthood), Water (east, infancy), Air (north, elder), and Fire (south, youth). These are the elements that sustain us. We are the cycles of the seasons, birth, growing up, maturity, old age and death. Our body is the container, composed of all four elements in a constant interchange, carrying us forward to our destinies.

The men I have been privileged to work with have taught me that the great movement of humanity to become more and more civilized has created a propensity toward dominance and the effort to control nature, isolate ourselves from it and to passively endorse what were once considered primitive notions that nature is evil and something to be subdued in the service of our cultural goals. This self-centered ethos has resulted in a super-individualism that feels no responsibility for anything other than its own gratification. Is it any wonder that we have difficulty agreeing? Even when we do recognize a social ill, acting on solutions is nearly impossible to coordinate. Even in respectful councils (of which I have been a part of hundreds) where the members have dedicated themselves to group and individual process and spirit through open and honest dialogue, it is difficult to reach agreement. I have come to the conclusion that the need for agreement before any forward movement can be made is an outdated model. It keeps old prejudices alive and perpetuates separation and conflict. To imagine there is an ultimate right and wrong, a right way or a wrong way to do anything, is the polarity of stagnation. Having opinions is another matter. We can all have our opinions. They are simply statements of where we stand on a certain question or principle. They are not, ideally, presented as absolutes, and are therefore open to dialogue and the possibility of supporting a decision that doesn't necessarily jive with our opinions.

If we turn to nature and the seasons that define it—and define human nature as well—we see a road map of evolution: the simple process of birth and growth, maturity and death. In human development we follow the basic four seasons. The human being does not remain static in one season, any more than the earth does. It can happen that large parts of ourselves remain in springtime, unable to mature because of profound wounds in childhood. Even so, the body goes on through the seasons to the eventuality of fall and winter. All the while, that in us which is stuck in a former season yearns to come along, to be healed and released so that we may live fully in the current season. Many of the men I have served, regardless of background, expend a great deal of effort untangling themselves from the overbearing voices and dominant attitudes that ensnare them in a disjointed reality. Many of the men have been imprinted to believe they are unworthy, and undeserving of beauty, meaning, joy. At a young age, as we discussed in the chapter on shadow and paradox, many forces come against our youth that cut down their budding spirits. They are implanted with the concept of scarcity, that there isn't enough and they must hoard and constantly drive on to obtain more wealth and comfort. Boys are already hard wired in their bodies to be focused on the survival of their people as a product of evolution that hasn't gone away. It should be no surprise to us that boys tattooed with the inscription of scarcity and the pride of accumulation would take on the giant of consumerism in a wrestling match. Too many of them are losing, broken badly in the lopsided match, because there is no vision inspired by a soulful connection with nature. My opinion.

It is more than opinion, however, when I consider the men and youth I have guided on solo fasting trips into nature. Something happens when we as humans bare ourselves to nature and walk into the dangerous and mysterious places with open hearts. Nature awaits us. It holds countless sacred places open for people who are willing to come. Nature knows us. As the story of the Northwest First Nation peoples says, "The forest knows where you are. If what a bird or a bush does is lost on you, then you are surely lost." There is accumulated wisdom in wild places that links in perfectly with our human chemistry, available with the exact fit to dock with our hearts and bring to life our inner truths. I have seen this work to perfection too many times to sit back and express myself with scholarly detachment. Men and youth come back from their prayer time in nature renewed, reborn and transformed. They come back having given birth yet again, as is the way of the soul, to undergo death and rebirth over and over in the course of a single lifetime. It is simply what we humans do. We are budding, growing beings. Destiny does not want to be bent by the forgetfulness of a self-serving culture based on isolationism and greed. It is clear by the degree of unhappiness and loneliness in our culture that our natural yearning for renewal is not being satisfied. I'm not making this up. Man after man has poured out his heart and expressed a profound soul hunger, a numb emptiness that is only made worse by models of success proffered by society. These men seek heart warmth and a soul home, because that is what constitutes a rich man.

I am reminded of a passage from Steven Foster and Meredith Little, who I have mentioned previously as teachers and guides of considerable duration. They bring men, women and youth out into deserts and woods for wilderness fasting to help them remember why they have come to their lives and how to live from their purpose. Upon returning from solo, participants often hear something like this from Meredith and Steven:

> Without a doubt, you have reason to fear. The world to which you return is far more savage, malicious, and defeating than the solitude and hunger of the threshold time. In the civilized world you must love and work and be responsible. You must somehow survive the routines, the pressures, the crises, the relationships, and all the future trials and tribulations of your new life station. You must nurture the flame of your purpose and carry its warmth to the most difficult corners. Above all, you must teach yourself to see that the civilized world is not only profane, but equally sacred.

Finally, one who is able to step outside his ordinary life, either by being in nature in solitude or through ritual and prayer, receives an unmistakable sense of being home. The settling in, nesting, grounding that takes place at these times feeds the buds of new potential. The grounded time and ritual solitude brings a great force of support, an experience of the soul team described in a previous chapter. In the safety of the soul team, one finds a flexibility in prayer that can be penetrated by grace, healing, and cleansing of anxiety and resentment. A vision begins to emerge of a more confident person who leaps into life, a gymnast sure of being spotted by the strong arms of meaning and purpose.

This reminds me of a man in Michigan, married with two children. He was in the midst of creating a consulting business designed to go into companies to help them improve their communication skills. He wanted to bring in a more heart-based style of interacting. To get it going he had spent nearly every penny he had. He loved his wife and children, and this whole idea had him deeply frightened. What was he doing? How could he risk the future of his children?

We were camped out in an eighty-acre hardwood forest and he took the risk of marking his vision and fear with ritual and prayer. He spoke his desire to the whippoorwills calling out in the darkness. He made a commitment to his vision, to what he imagined possible. He cut across what the logical mind might never have considered. He leapt to the next rung, trusting enough to believe he would catch a hold of what was next for him, that he and his family would survive.

Eight years later, his business has grown into a sort of community unto itself, providing enrichment for many business people who wouldn't have found a more fulfilling way without his vision. I'm not sure exactly how his declaration in the Michigan woods influenced the man's outcome, but I have no doubt it played a part. I haven't seen the concept better expressed than this passage from Goethe titled "Commitment:"

> Until one is committed, there is hesitancy, the chance to draw back, always ineffectiveness....But the moment one definitely commits oneself, then Providence moves too. All sorts of things occur to help one that would never otherwise have occurred. A whole stream of events issues from the decision, raising in one's favor all manner of unforeseen incidents and meetings and material assistance which no man could have dreamt would have come his way. Whatever you can do or dream you can, begin it. Boldness has genius, power and magic in it. Begin it now.

Have you ever been in a hardwood forest during a storm? With the fresh rain you can smell the decay, the moist rotting leaves, plants, wood, the essence and beauty of life and death living side by side. The hardwood trees, beech, oak, maple, elm and hickory all lean one way then the other in the wind. They resist only enough so they remain standing. You look up to see the sky blurred with the wind torn leaves and branches. Every so often the firecracker pop of a branch breaking shatters the air. In these storms I am struck by the way the trees appear to lean into the wind, into life. They are tested every season, by every sort of storm imaginable. Still, they lean into it, knowing they will be hurt, broken, scarred. The passionate forces will break off limbs, bend trunks, and the open wounds will call in carpenter ants that will chew on them and dismantle them bit by bit. Somehow, the trees become more beautiful with age. The more they are marked and broken, the more storied has been their leaning into life.

There are a few simple questions that men and women from

around the world often take with them into prayer and solo time in nature. These questions are as old as humanity and are asked not to find definite answers. The desire for answers is one of the modern traps we set for ourselves. It presumes an end, a conclusion, and so we sit and wait for it while the seasons of our short time on earth pass us by. The questions I'm referring to aren't meant to be answered for credit on a final exam. They are asked into the reflection of our individual soul waters. They show us illogical things, having to do with vision, destiny, service, evolution of spirit. For the most part, people for all of time and from every culture known to us have gone into solitude, nature and fasting with these basic questions. The men I have worked with will recognize them. I invite each of you to look them over. This version of the questions comes from Wayne Muller's book, *How, Then, Shall We Live.* I hope they can help you remember who you are, and appreciate yourself in the course of your evolving life:

1) Who am I? (How does my true nature unite me with all divine nature?)
2) What do I love? (What is at my center that fuels my inspiration, that touches me deeply?)
3) How shall I live knowing I will die? (How do I stay awake with the precious gift of time?)
4) What is my gift to the family of earth? (What gives meaning to my life?)[33]

Probably there are no answers that can be pinned down here. Yet the leaning into self, thus other, may be the only constant truth that man has ever known. The answers change each time the questions are asked, as it should be, constantly staying alive in the great art of humanity's unfolding nature.

Men have often ventured out away from comfort to create a separation from their ordinary lives, to consider the direction of one's life and his community needs and evolution. Who and what speaks from the solitude of the alone time often in wilderness settings. In this grounded, sensitively aware body inspiration, all sorts of benefit and support will come when a man steps into the reality of solitude.

Time and time again I have felt in myself and seen in others this cellular, elemental receptivity awaken in the body when wrapped in nature's diversity. It is as if in this separation there is a union with one's own soul, soul being thought by some to be the everlasting pool of grace and wisdom. Not to be taken for granted, for the soul does not sustain itself/ourselves without the nourishment of the creative journey of life-birth living and death.

In this solitude time, prayer time in receptive body awareness, we get an opportunity to interact with self, and other, all in the stew pot of an evolving, growing, empowering nature. Which, if I may say so, is this vast wealth of meaning which comes from being fully accepting and surrendering to one's own deeper engagement as an important and necessary creative expression of one's own very nature, and spirit and soul.

In all of this jargon there lies something that is wordless. It is the knowing sense, a sense deep in the belly for some of us. For others, it may be a whole body knowing. Each one of us knows the warm place inside that opens up when the meaning that nourishes is close at hand. We spring into life as a project of love, like a garden planted on a sunny day, ready for this nourishment that is the soul's fertilizer. We are poems written on a parchment of meaning, imbued by the happenings of life, the wedding of a friend, or an unexpected visit to the emergency room when a loved one has encountered a tragedy. Sometimes something almost beyond meaning arrives when you make love and it goes beyond the sex to another realm, weightless and calm in a mindless wonder.

It is not easy—not meant to be easy—this alone time, solitude, practice of letting communication flow without noise or human intervention that is so prevalent in the modern be-entertained-fast-association culture. Forces appear arrayed against our dropping into the quiet waters that are filled by our drinking of them. All the more reason to go there. All the more reason to fight through the bramble of logical and technological confusions that block our way. Something vital to the human race waits for us down there. It yearns for us as the mother whose son long gone at war has yet to return. We will find ourselves welcomed by the waters of solitude. There we will find rest, and the meaning we need to carry on. I urge you to find a quiet place, a time away from obligations, when you can listen to your heart voice. It will sing to you of your beauty, the beauty of your family, your people and a life lived in the holy ways.

6 Faith, Forgiveness, Reconciliation

WEST 01

Among the men I encounter, a common theme repeats. I've come to know it as a void in the personal structures of faith. I consider faith to be an unquestioning belief in one's purpose and the greater purpose of one's community. In these contemporary times, civilization has married itself to fast-paced individualism and its promise of happiness in material acquisition. The emptiness among men relates to emptiness in the current model—its tendency toward a lack of spiritual intimacy. In such a model it is difficult to have faith in one's self or anyone else.

In a milieu of faithlessness the power of forgiveness and reconciliation is diminished, if not lost entirely. How does one forgive or pardon when there is no position of acceptance upon which to stand? It doesn't seem possible to forgive and work out problems when there's no bedrock of meaning, when the fundamental attitude is that it doesn't matter. In such a condition a burden of unforgiveness weighs us down. We feel it as something heavy on us that we cannot shake—if we are alive enough to feel it at all. Anything resembling faith, and the sort of natural flow of faithful living, has no room to enter because of the heaviness of our resentments.

Perhaps a deeper truth in the unforgiveness of others is a fundamental hatred toward ourselves. In the soul work I have witnessed, it has become apparent time and again that underneath any hatred or harsh judgment is a similar feeling about ourselves. We know intellectually that to be human is to fail ourselves and others. No one is perfect, as the saying goes. Yet we struggle to find tolerance or mercy. Often, we make our guilt and shame into weapons. We spew out our distorted perceptions as some kind of psychic graffiti, defacing the beauty of our neighbors, our communities, our diversity. We can make such a mess of things from the certainty of judgements about *them* and all of their flaws. In the absence of faith, no force is there to guide us back to the teaching, to the self awareness available in reclaiming our judgments. The power of faithlessness increases its hold on us. The men I see carry it into our counsels as feelings of powerlessness, domination and a sense of being trapped in the traditional roles that crushed many of our fathers.

We grow into these roles in a process that in many ways looks like the opposite of growth, as if a young shoot, instead of growing toward the light, grows into a crack in the rock of darkness and twines in on itself until it has no way out. In the tightness of the role, the yearning heart has little access to the pools of soul and meaning that sustain us. In many ways, the knowledge of such pools is itself a myth, lost in the stream of uninitiated men pouring out of high schools and colleges with little to go on but the dog-eat-dog competitive bristle along the backs of their necks. Without faith, no measure of success is enough. A driven-ness to excess pushes our dementia for growth, as if that will fulfill us, when it is faith alone that offers peace. I see the desperation of this quandary in the sunken eyes and mistrustful expressions of the uniniti-ated unacknowledged men who through some act of God find their way to a gathering of brothers. Overwhelmed and frightened, yet consumed by a powerful longing, they often break down, and with rage and grief begin to understand the pain of their separation.

Men have been forced by the beast of material progress to cut out of their lives the time it takes to nurture a faithful life. We could debate ad infinitum how this has come about in the progression of human his-tory. When did it begin? With the planting of the first seeds of grain? The picking up of the first tool? The elevation of the first king or queen? The Industrial Revolution? I'm not in a position to analyze such things. All I know is that faith is a renewable resource, but it asks to be con-sciously acted upon through a daily practice. Otherwise, like so many of the tender virtues, it can wilt and die. In its absence, as men have taught me, hatred and rage take over the fallow pasture like a bindweed that leaves no room for other growth. As the great Persian poet Rumi says:

Out beyond ideas of wrong doing
and right doing,
there is a field. I'll meet you there.
When the soul lies down in that grass,
the world is too full to talk about.
Ideas, language, even the phrase "each other"
doesn't make any sense. [34]

It saddens me to say, or to perceive as I do, that we have lost our way to the field out beyond. Too often I hear frustrated men say things like, "Get over it," or, "That's just life," or, "What do you expect?" In these casual and pervasive comments, a kind of shame enforces the status quo, the "rightness" of this way over that. Men tell each other, in a form of helpless commiseration, to give up on having meaning and wonder in their lives. They bully each other into feeding their souls to the meat grinder of modern life. Underneath it an uninitiated rage smolders. Blame and harsh judgments predominate their landscape. Deep down nobody believes the lie. Deep down they know. It infuriates them. In the right environment the fury can become a great teacher. It can point the way to what needs healing, what needs clearing, what sort of ritual might provide entry to the wounds and to the reclaiming of one's soul. On the other hand, without a strong container, violence and destruction toward family, community and self, are the common manifestations of a faithless man's fury.

The strength to renew instead of destroy does not come easily. To repair bonds instead of ripping them apart is difficult if not impossible in a state of isolation and emptiness. Faith is a practice of degrees each day. It is a choice, upon rising out of bed, to be an advocate this day of generating life to its fullest beauty. It is the freedom to trust ancestry, trust humanity, god and spirit without having to resolve all of the dilemmas. Faith is an action, a decision to accept. The release into faith is a living prayer. Faith is the gateway to forgiveness, and thus the gateway to reconciliation.

In many ritual processes I have seen men face their pain, step into their rage and grief, blame and hostility, and realize in a moment of clarity how their damnation of others also damns them. We have known this as a culture for so long, and yet we continue to fall into the same trap. Matthew 7 states it so clearly: "Judge not, that ye not be judged. For with what ye judge, ye shall be judged: and what measure ye mete, it shall be measured to you again." Perhaps the forgetting and then remembering is an essential element of human evolution. Certainly it fits with the notion of forgiving ourselves. Whatever the path, it is clear to me that forgiveness and the taking back of our judgments has enormous power to heal. I do not consider it a casual act. Deep forgiveness requires a willingness to feel all of the feelings associated with whatever the transgression. It is not a brushing off in the manner of shooing a bothersome fly. The power of it lies in the depth to which it can take us to the place of knowing, after all is said and done, that there very well may have been nothing to forgive. In the depth of forgiveness, we can learn that what needed forgiving was that in us which presumed to know more than a brother or sister equally wise, or foolish. Here is the gateway to reconciliation in the most primary way. This is the time when a link is made between the other and us, and we can know serenity.

Still, in time we may forget we forgave, or be reminded anew of the old wound, and once again be called to the waters of forgiveness. The signs may arise as shortness of temper, a body sensation of jamming up, numbing out, shutting down, detaching, or a return to self-destructive compulsions. These indicators are asking to be tracked on a daily basis, and reconciled through acts of conscious interaction or the inner work of prayer, journaling or ritual process. There's no telling when an old wound we imagined to be healed will flair up and require attention again, and deliver to us a new layer of awareness. This is the organic nature of our changing existence. We are part of nature, held in the cycles of birth, maturation and death. Along the way, there are countless smaller versions of the cycles, the spontaneous rebirths, the sudden deaths, the unexpected pregnancies. We are reminded to be always ready to accept ourselves and others. Again and again, no matter the degree of difficulty, to allow forgiveness into our hearts. The alternative is to stay stuck in the chronic pain of unresolved grievances, to use blame and hatred in the form of a false healing salve, and convince ourselves we feel better at the expense of someone else.

These outward-directed illusions hold little promise of resolve. To actually move forward requires a deep commitment, to self and community. Some way of grounding into our human core provides the basis from which genuine resolution can take place. The way I've seen it work entails a naming process of behaviors and actions taken. Until we name things, they exist in a nebulous form, more ghost-like than real, and in that form, they haunt us. Naming is a practice of joining the ethereal with the material. In the material form of the name, whatever has happened, whatever the issue, we can look at it, feel it, and take ownership of our parts in it. From here, apologies, amends, understanding, forgiveness and reconciliation can ensue—a kind of soul fabric mending. In some cases, the mending is more specific to the heart fabric of emotional needs or wounds. Other times, a more complete soul damage, somehow deeper, is involved. In many cases, soul loss is at the core of what has happened. In a state of soul loss, a dimming of one's fire for life, a manner of being bothered, uptight, edgy, touchy, pervades the temperament. All sorts of damage to self and others comes from this internal disruption. Often, it goes back to primal wounds, trauma, some form of immature approach to survival that has grown into a barrier to full living. The deep healing of soul is a difficult, even lifelong, process. Some would say it takes many lifetimes.

What could be more important and yet so elusive? The reclaiming of and healing of soul…an indefinable feature, an energy, a presence, the life force of all life forces, our connection with the eternity that has come before us and after us. Soul joins us to the million-year human forum. Some say it reaches into the future, and connects us with the generations not yet born. The soul is ours to behold, while it also beholds us. It is not ours to be controlled. It belongs to itself, to its infinity. In some manner our bodies ingest it at conception and each cell is infused with it: our inheritance. It is like the best of friends or lovers. Soul is a force, the great mystery of evolution. Having always been, it is now in the form of human life, in the body—its lover the body. From an awareness of soul comes faith in soul, an understanding of the self evolution we all undergo. In faith we can lean into life, lean into the soul purpose and become the beauty of our soul's longing, become the yearning for that beauty.

In so many men's stories I discover again and again the separation of soul from everyday life. A gap or veil creates an impasse and it becomes difficult, and feels impossible to live a life of meaning and purpose. This impasse prevents reconciliation between the conflicting forces of soul and ego, between the sacred and the mundane. I, and so many of my brothers, walk around in a state of agitation from this unresolved division within ourselves. When the connection is brought back together, something beautiful happens.

Often times at a gathering, jam sessions erupt in between regular activities. Someone picks up a drum, another man a flute. Others begin clapping, chanting, singing. A couple of men start growling and wrestling, rolling in the soft green grass and dandelions. A natural pride of sheer existence envelops us. Over there a man who has been pensive, wrapped tight and unable to let go, suddenly bursts into an exuberant cavorting movement across the meadow. He may be a man who has been afraid to dance for fifty years, who has imagined himself uncoordinated, or disinterested, too serious with the weight of his responsibilities to partake of frivolous play. Taken by the magic of a moment in-between, his suppressed freedom leaps into the air without a care of how he is perceived, how he looks, or whether it is right or wrong. His hips oiled by the joy that comes when he is connected to his eternity, he boogies like someone on a street corner with a boom box. All of his ideas about what a man is supposed to be like, how he is supposed to act, fall away as a skin too small to contain him.

Too often many of us forget this kind of exuberance. We live in a self-imposed exile, a shallow suffering that shows up as irritability, finding fault in others or "society," grousing and complaining about how screwed up everything is. The image I have is of a man whose arms and legs are encased in blocks of ice. He cannot move. Does he do anything about getting himself out of his predicament? Sometimes. Usually, he looks around him and sees what's wrong with everyone and everything else, imagining the problem is out there. The problem, however, is right there with him. He doesn't have the soul fire to melt his frozenness. The more he complains, the more he chokes off oxygen to the soul and the more it smolders. It is difficult to create beauty from this position, and it has been said that beauty is what attracts God. Without beauty, we do not experience grace, and so the situation worsens. In an exhausted state, the life force nearly snuffed, the idea of having a genuine purpose all but vanishes.

A turning point can come when a man allows himself to deeply feel his genuine state of being. If he can come to terms with his suffering, call in some support through prayer, the beginnings of reconciliation can occur. One of the key elements seems to be a willingness to take responsibility for his lot in life. We have such a culture of victimization and blame, always looking for whose fault it is and how much we can sue them for. There's nowhere to go from this position. All the power lies outside with whoever we have identified as our persecutor. Claiming responsibility, taking ownership, is also taking back the power. Unexpected transformations can spontaneously take place. A family history that appeared so terrible, so unimaginably cruel, suddenly appears okay, as it was meant to be. Childhood defeats and the losses of a lifetime no longer appear as failures, but are seen as teachers and are appreciated. Now seems like a good place to insert one of my favorite poems. It fits here, but it is so rich, it could go anywhere, anytime. It was created by Rainer Maria Rilke, translated by Robert Bly:

A Man Watching

I can tell by the way the trees beat, after
so many dull days, on my worried windowpanes
that a storm is coming,
and I hear the far-off fields say things
I can't bear without a friend,
I can't love without a sister.

The storm, the shifter of shapes, drives on
across the woods and across time,
and the world looks as if it had no age:

the landscape, like a line in a psalm book,
is seriousness and weight and eternity.

What we choose to fight is so tiny!
What fights with us is so great!
If only we would let ourselves be dominated
as things do by some immense storm,
we would become strong too, and not need names.

When we win it is with small things,
and the triumph itself makes us small.
What is extraordinary and eternal
does not want to be bent by us.
I mean the Angel who appeared
to the wrestlers of the Old Testament:
when the wrestlers' sinews
grew long like metal strings,
he felt them under his fingers
like chords of deep music.

Whoever was beaten by this Angel
(who often simply declined to fight)
went away proud and strengthened
and great from the harsh hand,
that kneaded him as if to change his shape.
Winning does not tempt that man.
This is how he grows: by being defeated decisively,
by constantly greater beings. [35]

In the true understanding of one's defeats as the greatest teachers, the internal conflicts of a lifetime can begin to loosen. There is a physical sensation associated with this, as if a festering wound has been cleansed and bandaged, an inflammation of the skin treated and calmed. A false sense of inflation, the grandiosity of a narcissistic sufferer, lessens like the decreased swelling of a twisted joint. The men who have reached such places of resolve have taught me that it is possible to move from dissonance to consonance, from stew pot to rendered essence, to the meaning at the heart of life through the process of engaged humanity. And conflict, irritation, projection, hatred and harsh judgment are where the unexpected seeds of beauty wait for the soul gardener to hoe furrows *in himself.*

In this way the disorienting energies become guideposts. They call us to the path of life that wants our shadows to be brought out of the oppressed state of the unknown. These eruptions and inflammations that may appear as unfair plagues are stories waiting to be told, allowed, accepted and honored so that the meaning of life can be illuminated through them. Then we can all receive their teachings. Our communities need to hear our stories, and when we go inside and reclaim them, something of importance happens on a scale larger than ourselves.

To leave unreconciled difficulties and unresolved conflicts, is to pass onto our children the unfinished soul work of our life's beauty. This is how prejudice, futility, isolation and many other forms of soul disconnection get a hold of our youth. It is the responsibility of mature adults to show faith through their actions. Our guidance comes from the practice of recovering our ancestral blood and wisdom, and remembering the ancient ways of moving through the hatred, the conflict, the tendency toward mammalian. So many spiritual traditions and the work of so many poets and artists tells us the truth of such a practice. It is a truth as important as life itself. Let us turn to these elders who tell us that what happens *after* conflict matters more than the conflict. How we deal with the breakdown, the hurt or the misunderstanding reveals whether or not something has been learned and what our dedication is to the relationship and the community. What we do afterward is a statement of our faith. Let us remember our tendency to wound each other, and ourselves, and open ourselves to the equal tendency to heal, like the body's natural and immediate work to repair a fractured bone. The disappointments, losses and hurts of living, the broken bones and cuts that leave scars, are the ways nature uses us as a canvas. This becomes our beauty. This is essential to who we are, just as the lightning scar on the trunk of an old tree tells of a great storm endured. To be defeated, as

Rilke says, and survive to walk with the wound in dignity, just as the tree, though beaten, still reaches for the sun—is the stuff of a great life.

If we aren't willing to work with the messiness, we miss the most important opportunities to grow. How we handle our difficulties is the sustaining force of humanity. All of us everywhere have this in common: the regenerating power of forgiveness. It is easy to imagine ourselves powerful when everything is going smoothly, or to imagine ourselves arrived when we are disengaged from the struggle. The times when defeat appears unavoidable have the potential to bring us truly to ourselves, to the divine connections between us. To repeat the First Nation prayer from the Yaqui tradition: "I am another you, you are another me." How might an understanding of this prayer influence our approach to conflict? It tells us that the veil between people, the subject/object construct, is something of a lie. Once again we are reminded of the human paradox: our position between two worlds, individuals and yet merged with a greater whole. Certainly these understandings express the brotherhood and sisterhood among us. They remind us of our commonality and of our capability to enact the worst of human traits, or the most graceful.

In the work I have done these last fifteen years, conflict has come up at almost every gathering. In fact, my colleagues and I think of conflict as a barometer: when conflict doesn't arise, we get nervous. It is the container with conflict under the surface that has the degree of pressure necessary for an explosion. Contrary to some of our utopian ideals, the group without conflict, the one that appears most at peace, is usually the most suspect...and the most dangerous. So I must admit that I am relieved when conflict comes to the surface. I can't deny that it is charged, volatile and sometimes frightening. When it is embraced and engaged in honestly, however, truth is rendered up to consciousness. Those who seemingly want to fight become mirrors for one another. What appeared at first as difference often becomes similarity, and we realize that our judgment of another is actually something we don't like in ourselves.

In this dance with paradox, our individuality, the undeniable alchemical and vibrational differences between us, sets us up for conflict with each other, while at the same time opening a gateway to our unity. Such a strange contradiction that is just as is should be. So much the way of people.

I believe that in time science will understand what the indigenous cultures have known for eons: we are all related. Any act of violence, any conflict, regardless of who is right or wrong, says just as much about us as individuals than the other persons. Somehow we learn the most when we stop believing our projections, our tendency to make objects out of people or issues, and stop seeing only that which separates us. An orientation toward our unity can stop brutality from being wreaked on our so-called enemies, and stop the destruction being brought upon the earth.

In our society the youth learn to not trust. They are taught to be suspicious of people who are different—different belief systems, different colors, customs and structures. Rather than teaching tolerance or fostering appreciation of other ways, we foment an attitude of scorn, as if the other way is somehow inferior, and the people are of less value than "us." By the time we are adults many of us are cemented into our beliefs. Faith, forgiveness and reconciliation have little room to live in the human psyche with such hardened truths about others.

In my work I have witnessed men, women and youth engage in the healing process in many ways. The wisdom of these vital souls has taught me that conflict has a better chance of working out if it is wrapped in a prayerful, grounded container. When the ancestors and helping spirits are invoked, it is more likely that individuals will let go of their entrenched positions. Prayer becomes a means of grounding and a channel for the allies. The helping spirits are standing by, always, awaiting our call and our invitation to help. Some say this of our ancestors: they want nothing more than to serve us, to aid us in reaching reconciliation and achieving resolve. As a witness in hundreds of circles where prayer and invocation have been activated, I have come to a deep respect for the value of such practices. Something happens that couldn't have taken place without the aid of our circles, both seen and unseen. I have felt deep in my soul that prayer has unlimited applications in the support of healing and vision for humanity.

A simple model for resolving conflict was shown to me by Cliff

Barry and Tom Daly (see page 181), I have worked with it and seen its effectiveness on numerous occasions. In its basic form it looks like this: Two people face each other, having agreed to work on whatever issue separates them, and willing to move the energy out of themselves and into a realm where what *truly* wishes to be expressed can come forward. They speak to the following questions:

1) What do I feel? That is, what is my emotional state: angry? hurt? surprised?

2) What were the details? What exactly happened? For example: When you hung up the phone on me... When you pushed me... When you laughed at me... etc.

3) What are my judgments? For example: I judge that you don't have time for me... It's my judgment that you don't respect me.

4) And the final question, What do I want? For example: I want to know if my judgment is true... I want an apology...I want you to stop doing that.

The final question is an invitation to renewal, a request to work it out. Often we will not get what we want. We are asked to accept the outcome, and to realize that being engaged in the process itself is huge soul-healing work. When the first person is done speaking his answers to these questions, the other speaks back what he heard. In this way, the originator knows he has been fully listened to. He has the opportunity to clarify if a point is misconstrued, or to reiterate if something important is missing. With the mirroring complete, the roles switch and the other individual speaks his answers to the questions. The listener then repeats back what he heard, again clarifying and refining the information so that it feels correct. Several times of back and forth may be necessary to reach a point of completion for both parties. Often this four step process takes place with witnesses present, who are asked to practice neutrality, and with a facilitator to help keep the process on track.

A prayerful container for such work often deflates, to a degree, the aggressive tendencies that come out of conflict in its early stages. Something about the process and the witnessing circle—both of living bodies and of the spirit team and the ancestors—slows down the urge to strike out, and removes the conflict from linear time. At times it is necessary to let the incident rest for a little while before going into this process, or to dissipate some anger by giving it to the earth. Most of us know that time heals, and sometimes taking a five minute walk before engaging in a conflict can prevent excessive wounding. Whatever the approach, it has become clear to me these tools, or others like them, are invaluable in reaching healthy resolutions to conflict. Of course their success is dependent on both parties being willing to work together. It also takes time to learn the model. An openness to making mistakes, and allowing for some sloppiness at first, is necessary. Nothing teaches like real life practice. I encourage people to give it a try. Find helpers, mediators or guides when possible. But try. It won't take long to recognize the vast potential.

I realize this is asking a lot. It's something with which we are unfamiliar. Reconciliation, while coming more into practice lately, is still a rather uncommon experience. It involves faith, a deep trust in ourselves, our people, our gods. The willingness to try is true courage, a personal testament to a deep belief in the meaning and value of life. It is not easy. Many of us have been traumatized in explosive conflicts where we had no power. Childhood wounds resurface when conflict arises, and we go into a sort of shock, a shutdown, even terror. Then there is a tendency to avoid conflict, to not speak up, become a doormat, or a rager who explodes after he or she can't take it anymore. In general, it appears, our culture prefers to gloss over the natural friction of living. As Rilke says, the result of avoiding a wrestling match with the angel of the Old Testament is a certain shallowness. When we avoid conflict, we avoid the depth of human passion and pain, and we are the lesser for it. Often, the relationship that doesn't fight lacks a degree of love, a richness of texture, the nuance of being bent by a great storm and surviving. If we do not own our aggressions, and learn how to reap the great teachings of our enemies—even if, in the moment, the face we most despise is our wife, child, friend—we risk losing each other, and ourselves.

One of the great losses of our times, I believe, and a huge factor affecting our ability to peacefully resolve conflict, is the loss of our elders. It is traditional for the elders to guide the people through their disagreements. They are the ones who have passed through the years of striving and can hold our crises with the hands of time. They can lead us to the wisdom inherent in conflict. The elders can help us see the breath of life that issues from our good fights, and the way it feeds the community, heals and matures the soul.

In olden times the elders held the faith. They knew the power of persevering through our difficulties. They knew how such dedication delighted the ancestors and attracted Spirit. We don't live with the elders anymore, and that breaks my heart. My prayer is that men and women of conscience come into their elderhood in full awareness, with a practice of such ways well under their belts, and rekindle the place of active elderhood in our communities. It does no good to bemoan what has gone wrong. See it, yes. Name it, for sure. And then move in, take it into the body cavity, claim it as our own and enable the transformation.

The light you give off
did not come from a pelvis.
Your features did not begin in semen.
Don't try to hide inside anger
radiance that cannot be hidden.   —Rumi

THE PATH OF INQUIRY AND ITS RELATIONSHIP TO MATURITY
inherently involves opening oneself to deep emotional energies. It is our
feelings that inspire us to live with vision and to heal whatever blocks us
from full living. It is this energetic exchange between components and
qualities of our being that brings us health and well being on many levels. The emotions serve as initiators and guides that report to us on the
state of our life's pilgrimage. They alert us to impending change and
speak to us of our resistance and its source. They tell us whether or not
our current lifestyle serves our soul purpose, our reason for being. The
practice of listening to these voices and feeling these energies then
becomes a central act in the daily process of personal evolution and the
lifelong initiatory journey.

I have noticed over the years how some men who come to various
councils and gatherings are packed with suppressed emotions. A kind of
personal oppression holds the feelings in check, like angry guard dogs
that attack the self if the emotions attempt to escape, and also attack
friends and family if they get too close to the prisoners. It becomes
almost impossible to access these imprisoned feelings. Without that
opportunity our radiance is most often diminished. Maintaining stasis
requires incredible energy. The force pushing outward comes from biological and ancestral memory of a natural opening to the soul's story, the
natural wish to accept an honorable position in the community.

Keeping it down is so very difficult, and yet it is the norm in modernity to do so.

Even though imprisoned, the emotions maintain a voice and occupy a place inside of us as if they were literally embodied. To enjoy health requires some ability to bless our emotional bodies and reconcile with them. By listening to them we can learn when despair, resentment, rage or confusion have consumed us. They inform us that it is time to pray, to connect with Spirit, to release the forces that hold us in check and learn from the story of our lives. Teaching and healing come when a community gathers and places the emotions into a ritual container. It is a strong container that makes it okay for the hardest feelings to emerge. I have witnessed the power of such events on many occasions, and have experienced the molecular healing, deep and biological, that circulates through all of those gathered—not just the individual who is the focus.

This is the beauty and magic of ritual time, or dream time, that can be opened by those humble enough to allow the worlds of conscious and unconscious to meet where the physical and the spiritual can mingle. In the meeting, a dialogue ensues that is of great benefit to both worlds. In the dialogue, the soul receives water, like spring rains in the desert, and flowers bloom that haven't been seen for generations. Their sudden beauty opens us to the soul's meaning and purpose, and something close to peace quiets the nervous mind. I experience these times of convergence as a salve applied to troubles, to despair and grief. The ritual serves as a soul midwife, who opens the lid of these salves, invites us to lean back and to feel our belonging, relax into place and being, where all of our feelings enjoy safety and can come forth in their purity.

In some cases this takes the form of the ridiculous, and is no less profound than any other manifestation of the divine. As I have said before, humor is major ingredient in ritual when the tension becomes too great and the ritual takes itself too seriously. One of my favorite experiences of this has been the ongoing emergence of Shecky, a shadow character of my dear friend and colleague, Keith Fairmont.

As I look back on it, the crack in reality that allowed Shecky to come out in all his glory came one night at a gathering around a fire deep in a Colorado canyon. It was during our soul-based Men's Leadership

Training Program, a week-long encampment to support men in their purpose and to honor their journey, their visions, and to renew their hearts and souls. As we stood around the fire during a ritual dance, a clown came forward, stripped off his pants and threw them in the fire. Unbeknownst to him, there were two butane lighters in the pockets. During the clown's routine at the fire pit his pants suddenly exploded, sending soot and coals flying in all directions, then exploded with equal drama a second time. Several men dove for cover shouting, "Incoming!"

Suddenly the clown's show had gotten bigger than him, and the explosion of gas brought an explosion of laughter even more dramatic. The amount of bottled tension freed in us that evening would be impossible to measure, but the relief and freedom, the lightness that followed, has been a gift to us all that has lasted literally years. The hole that was blown open that night became the birth canal for the stand-up comic, Shecky (named after the old master of one-liners, Shecky Green).

Shecky didn't come out right away, but waited a year. At the next Leadership Training he arrived next to the same fire pit wearing the mask of a bum smoking a cigar. He began to lampoon one of America's biggest shadows   that of the greedy businessman who will take advantage of anything that happens in order to make a buck. Shecky began enlisting men in his mythical deal, having to do with the buying and selling of some imaginary product never quite defined. It was all about the deal, a ludicrous, maddening obsession to make everyone buy something they absolutely had to have but could not be told what it was. Those who resisted Shecky's pitch were subject to a merciless barrage of insults and put downs designed to manipulate them into doing exactly what Shecky wanted them to do.

All the demons that haunt modern man were rolled into this absurd character, who was loud and obnoxious and hilarious. No one was safe from him. He pointed out to each of us what cowards we were, what fools we were for believing in all of our own little schemes, our own foolish desires to "get ahead," make it happen, to be movers and shakers. No one could help but release to some degree the iron grip he had on his version of Shecky—the vaudeville of his attempts to get ahead in the world at all costs.

At times Shecky grew to monstrous proportions, and was himself taken prisoner by the all-consuming American imperative to be successful, to attain wealth and power at all costs. Some men no doubt wanted to throw *him* in the fire, to escape what had become far too real and frightening. Then he would deliver a one-liner to his side-kick Frankie and we would all be in stitches.

Throughout the week, Shecky popped in at the most unexpected times: during a meal, after a council, while we were playing football in the meadow. He was the perfect example of shadow energy, how it can leap up at us when least expected, at the moment when we feel most "together," and remind us of our humanity, our weakness, our silliness, our limitations. Shecky was one of those characters that most certainly altered Keith, his creator, but also altered every man who experienced his cigar-smoking wheeling and dealing. His was beautiful and grotesque and one of the most interesting pieces of ritual process I have ever witnessed.

So much of life calls out to be honored and celebrated in ritual and healed by the soul doctor. The passages of child to adult, adult to elder, elder to death and death to spirit; the times of wedding, divorce, disease, struggle and all the feelings of grief, anger and loss find their voices in ritual, the place in which the unknown and less tangible structures of our lives feel at home. This is the dwelling of our ancestors, our allies and helping spirits. They know the ways of non-ordered states of being, the connections and avenues of contact that serve the people. Indigenous peoples all around the world understand this, and know from experience that rituals are hollow without the presence of the ancestors. They know that it goes both ways, that our ancestors also benefit and are healed by our rituals.

One of the most powerful examples of this is when a father and son do a reconciliation and marking ritual in a circle of men. The arena is defined by the dreams and prayers of the gathering. Father and son can step into this arena and sit in the center of this circle where an altar or shrine has been built with each man's personal objects. The father, who is naturally much closer to death, and the son much closer to birth, come together on the neutral ground, often after years of estrangement.

A question is asked of them: What from the past wishes to be spoken to? What forgiveness or truth saying needs to be laid with the other holy objects on the shrine? What in the present moment, from your intuitive self, wishes to be acknowledged and marked and witnessed in this circle? What vision, dream or hope do you have for yourself and each other as you cast your heart toward the future?

The father is asked to speak first, as the elder, even if it is his son who asked him to come. Often he begins with the story of his grandfather and father, their ancestors. The truth begins to unfold, with the beauty of a fiddle head fern in the spring unfurling itself to reveal its delicate and fragile beauty. Like the fern, the story is edible and nutritious to the souls of all who witness and are fed by it.

In that moment the father can reveal his greatness and own his mistakes, and ask for forgiveness. It becomes clear that all fathers wound their sons. Jungian analyst James Hillman has said it is even a father's duty.

Often the father moves into the future, asks his son to walk with him at his side, that they enjoy the life that is left for them to share. By this time most of the men in the room are in tears, if not sobbing. To witness this brings the healing salve of grief—honored, acknowledged and spoken.

We then turn toward the son and the same questions are asked of him. Even though he has had less opportunity to be defeated, he most often rises to the occasion and understands from his heart and soul that his father did the best he could, as all the fathers did before him. The father and son are then asked to rise and embrace, to begin anew the precious gift of their short lives together.

These father and son rituals are an example of the incredible emotional charge attached to our core relationships. When given an outlet set in ritual context, the intuitive powers of the men come forth in dramatic ways. Being held and witnessed blooms the possibility of healing, not only for those in the center, but for all of us around. It defines the choice we all have in defining our futures, laying a foundation for deeper intimacy wherever we find ourselves.

Something about these father and son rituals travels back through the lineage, back into time as the pages of a book being rapidly flipped by a sure breeze. There is music: songs of rejoicing heard in the hearts of those who are present, coming to the ears of intuition from spirits of the past. Some would say there is no greater gift one can give to his people than to heal a current relationship that in turn brings a healing back to the springs from which we originally arose, and forward into future generations.

For many of us in the modern world, such notions are strange, foreign and suspect. To give blessings or even acknowledge past generations appears as a threat to current accomplishment and the individualistic temperament that demands credit, a feeling of autonomy or heroic recognition. Somehow we have gotten the idea that our inventions make us superior to those who came before us. We celebrate the latest improvement of the microchip without any thought of what it is built upon, its origin with the first humans to carve out symbols in the walls of caves, the first silicon chip, that was broken off the edge of a stone used for scraping animal hides. I don't quite understand this orientation, and find it odd that we can live so selfishly, cut off from our roots as we are, and not even seem to notice. The current forward-leaning orientation has become so dominant the very idea of serving our ancestors appears absurd. People might ask: What do ancestors have to do with the Dow Jones index? How are they going to get me that 5,000 square foot house? And so we lean forward, push hard at the future with sharp desire, and the past is little more than an annoyance, like a cord tied to a spear that holds it back from its penetrating aims.

If we never leave the dominant reality, nothing can challenge it. The way it is will be the way it is. If we risk leaving the ways of mainstream society behind, however, and enter the natural world, slow down and remember the smell of the elements, a different sort of yearning begins to emerge. It happens slowly for some, instantly for others. Nature in its wisdom breaks down the resistance to soul, one's own and the collective soul. A different form of wisdom comes forward. Slowly, the messengers invoked at the start of a gathering—the helping spirits of ancestors, allies, the local geography—begin to show up. They provide unexpected support in the form of hunches, intuitions, and sometimes great epiphanies. The possibility of healing, vision, the breaking free of stuckness, confusion, destructive repetitions, becomes real in the sacred container of ritual, infused with helping ancestral spirits. Most men yearn for freedom, a sense of having their spirits not penned in from excessive responsibilities. What I continually find is that most men can access this quality of freedom in ritual process, in the simple practice of any form of awareness which includes prayer.

Still, it is often a battleground, even in well built ritual containers, between the forces of resistance, logical programming, the arrogance of modern empiricism and the intangible, whimsical, ethereal, indirect elements of ritual and soul. Perhaps I too am trapped by my thought processes, my own judgments, but it seems clear we are groomed primarily to dominate. We thrive on the language of conquest. Winning is what matters, and it is the winning, as the poet Rilke says, that makes us small. We don't seem to recognize how this attitude isolates us from the most essential connections of life, or how our quest for salvation in the material world alone prevents us from receiving the true richness we long for.

I have seen it so many times. Men show up at gatherings beaten up and drained by the pressures of modern living. Rarely do they arrive in the joy of a full heart and soul richness. Their appearance, underneath a robust and well fed exterior, is of lean wolves who get by on tiny scraps of grace, little, sometimes barely noticed, intimations of hope. These they hold in their cheeks like wads of chewing tobacco, the bitter taste of someday, maybe, all of this will satisfy me.

This is how I experience the loss of spiritual community among the men with whom I work. It is the pain of backward initiation, what happens when passages are not marked and honored. If we do not consciously pass through, the threshold becomes an oven and the initiation a protracted baking. I speak of these things not to lay blame. I realize that throughout this book I have criticized our modern ways, at times have made the very mistakes I warn against. Nevertheless, I cannot deny what fifteen years of work has taught me: we have lost our way. The detours from human evolution on a heart and soul level have cost us dearly.

What seems normal in current times is the pathway of control. Man has altered his relationship to the earth under the assumption he can control the earth's cycles, which is a complete turnaround from earlier more soulfully connected times when man realized he was of the earth and could not separate himself from it. We have nurtured a false truth that has dangerously inflated us. In our separation from nature, both inner and outer, we have become lost in the illusion of superiority. But as Rilke says, that which is extraordinary and eternal does not want to be bent by us. In the practice of attempting to bend and bind the greatness of the earth, we have unknowingly created a monster of vast proportions that, in truth, dominates and controls us. In this state of slavery, we go about our happy servitude ignorant to the losses we have endured, stripped of our meaning and purpose, our ancestral wisdom and the richness that has sustained humanity for millions of years. The monster of our arrogance doesn't allow prayer and ritual. The old ways of healing, the expression of emotions into rich beds of compost that break them down into soul food, are lost to many of us. I don't have to tell you the consequences of suppressing soul evolution. Anyone who notices can see how thirsty kindness has gotten.

Since 1986 I have witnessed and supported hundreds of men through prayer and ritual, through fasting and solitude. One of the core desires among those I have encountered, if not the most central, is to find their soul home, to find the sense of self as home, the sense of place in the world and deep body meaning. The same basic urge has been consistent among men, women, and the youth with whom I have worked. Included in the core desire, very close to it, perhaps a Siamese twin, is a sense of worthiness and the practice of self-love. The awakenings that occur in this work almost always have to do with men living out of their creative inspiration and intuitions, which leads them to service and generativity in their communities and a love for the earth. It is about men knowing their own sense of grace and grounded manhood. It leads inevitably to an appreciation of ancestors, their sacrifices, and to an experience of personal holy energy or power in the world, the importance of evolving, growing, initiating and healing in the pilgrimage throughout life.

The vehicle to such knowledge is often through the emotions, or the feeling states. Passion and desire, dreams and visions are the tools. If we are receptive, the feelings provide us with information. I sometimes

think of it as a Geiger counter, this receptivity. There's an audible click-
ing that can tell us where there is danger or interest or need. The practice of receptivity, as in the feminine body of a man, can and will lead
to refinements, capacities and the ability to receive a broader range of
signals. It has been said that in olden times, the senses were known to
be many more than five—something like eight or ten, even twelve. We
can begin to comprehend such a range of sensation through the practice of internal listening. Slowly, the small voices of intuition, hunch
and presentiment can be heard. Some of the First Nation peoples have
said these are the voices of the ancestors coming to help us. These allies
who dwell in the spirit world, some say, are waiting to help us bloom
and blossom throughout our lives.

I received an early lesson in this at the very first men's retreat we
put together outside of Colorado in 1989. The gathering was to take
place in a hardwood lot in north central Michigan. We arrived five
hours early to set up and there was already a truck parked off the road.
We couldn't imagine who would be there so early.

The conditions were the worst possible to set up a camp for thirty-
five men: rain and mud. I carried a load of tarps and tents down into a
clearing. My face dripped with rain. From out of the woods walked a
First Nation man, stocky with an angular face and beautiful long dark
hair. He looked at me and then up at the teeming sky and asked point
blank, "Didn't you pray?"

It's humorous now, looking back on it, but at the time I wanted to
drop all of the gear, fall to my knees and admit my ignorance. "No," I
wanted to say, "I didn't pray." I didn't even know *how* to pray for the
rain to stay away. I remember feeling instantly stripped, a fool caught
unprepared, unmasked, who had no business thinking he could guide a
Spirit weekend.

What I learned from that time was how important it is to consciously tend to my personal receptivity and feeling energies in advance
of any work I intend to do. At that weekend, we were so focused on the
details and the necessary logistics of camp that we hadn't prepared the
soul ground in the ways that were needed. That man's question, though
painful to hear, taught me that preparation for a gathering has as much

to do with preparing the soul, the inner camp of feelings, as it does with the actual physical space (and it might have rained anyway). It has become clear to me that authentic inner preparation affects positively the physical components of the gathering. When the soul is informed and the heart open and receptive, set up and tear down of camp goes smoothly and is not seen as extra work, but an essential element of completing the circle.

When we cultivate our feeling receptivity, what has been called the valley spirit that yields and receives into itself through patience and openness, our intuitive life is waiting to serve us. It is waiting to help us heal, enjoy our passions, find the meaning and soul home for which we yearn. This is a capacity we all have—men and women, children and elders. The children, in fact, can be our best teachers. They haven't had their files packed with information like the adults and have a natural receptivity that is innocent and true. We can all cultivate the intuitive realm. Most of us, unfortunately, have never been encouraged to do so.

I look to a reawakening of these powers. They can save our lives. When there are important decisions to be made, that intuitive energy is there to serve us, if we will allow it. For the most part, however, we are blocked from this vital support. It saddens me. The linear, logical thinking aspects that have been reinforced and locked in by a culture of conquest, push out the less complicated, simple wisdoms. It has the effect of cutting us off from our roots, our native wisdom and blood memories—the truths that don't require proving.

My questions to you are these: What are your current emotional states? Are they giving birth to your life? Are they encouraging you to resolve any unfinished business with another person? Are they signifying that you are going through a rite of passage, shedding an old way of being so that you are ready for a new opportunity? Are your feelings informing you of some energy that is suppressed? of a joy that has no voice? nowhere to dance? or some imbalance in the circle of your life, possibly inhibiting your evolution?

An elder once told me that we are always in the process of becoming. What he spoke of was the daily practice of connecting to Spirit and our organic life as it works toward its potential. The backdrop to this, what we come up against often, are culturally reinforced logical thought processes that leave out heart and soul needs. The result of this is a society based on self-centered needs, always fearful of losing the cherished object and driven to tenacious pursuit. This way of being inherently cuts us off from the meaning of our spiritual selves and our communities. We are left with an overworked, angry nation compelled to feed its soul with material goods—the survival of the richest. That these ways do not satisfy is common knowledge to anyone who has developed some of the receptivity I am referring to.

The world community tells us our way is not working. There are more divorces, more violence, human rights abuses, slaughters in high schools, more people depressed and on medication than ever before. The evidence can be difficult to hear, yet we must not stay in denial. I don't mean to say there aren't skillful people and programs working to address these issues. More and more there is help emerging. Even if every tree in the forests of the world was cut down, there would still be pockets of warmth in the human kindness and beauty that is always present. Many people want to do good by our children and elders. I'm more concerned with dominant culture, the tide if you will, the undertow that takes down the youth and sweeps them out to sea unprepared or empowered to mature into healthy adults who have been touched by the wisdom of the elders. It will take many generations, I believe, to reconcile the damage that has been done. A huge part of that work will come to bear when the elders are loved back into overseeing the human heart and soul. So often it is their caring that fuels the inspiration to participate fully.

What calls to me is some form of bending back to the true and basic wisdoms of humanity. Perhaps it is more of a bending inward, to the core of our natural ways, the power of love to guide and inspire us. In this way we can rediscover the true richness of living, where the joy of heart and soul thrives. Another elder, many years ago, came up to me after a town meeting and said, "True rage creates possibilities. False rage destroys." Too much is being destroyed on earth these days by this false rage. It comes from an inward twisted energy that has gotten confused, unable to find the natural channel for expression, and turns in on itself, as a form of self hatred or masochism. It lives in the body as a loaded gun ready to go off at the slightest provocation. These feelings grind at our stomachs like chunks of gristle that cannot be digested. Like all emotions, when rage is not allowed a healthy expression, witnessed and blessed, the energy cannot dissipate. It builds. The pressure grows. At this point, it can link into archetypal energy forms, what some would term evil, and can be unconscionably destructive, of others first, then itself. Nature will eventually eliminate it, as it does all powers that no longer serve, but the cost is great.

One of the forums we have created for the free expression of emotions is called Spirit Camp, or Spirit and Soul Retreat. When I say free, I don't mean free in the sense of irresponsibility. The freedom we encourage, what we call "radical freedom," has a basis in the truth of a mutual understanding that our forms of expression must be sensitive to the others present. Still, there is a danger here, always the potential for crossover, when one man's freedom feels to another man like oppression. When conflict arises, the participants have an agreement to work it out honorably. As midwives, we establish the container—define the ritual space complemented and strengthened by helping spirits, our ancestors and the land itself. Everything else that happens, for the most part, is up to the participants.

I have experienced countless men's retreats. It is difficult to convey in words the essence of these retreats. They are gatherings in the non-logical world of ritual and prayer. The men who come seek their authenticity, and open themselves to the mystery. They step into the creation of living the moment-to-moment art that is their lives. In the fullness of respected place, we explore the art of manhood, the art of humanity, what it means to know worthiness, be inspired, and find our ways of service. The gatherings are spontaneous and organic, directed by Spirit, through the ancestors and natures of the men and the place. We open ourselves to the many pathways to God, what Joseph Campbell calls the "Hero with a Thousand Faces," [36] and we seek our deep meaning together. At all the gatherings we strive to recognize each man's voice as equally important. Many religious forms are represented—all are welcome and encouraged.

The men who have come are there to experience the complexities of who they are and to behold their brothers. Each of us is a teacher, in the sense described in Susan Trott's wonderful book *The Holy Man*,[37] in which the holy man's basic teaching is to see each person we encounter as a holy man or woman. We give ourselves to the never ending becoming of who we are and who we are meant to be. What takes place is art—an honorable practice of creating that will never be finished.

Men come together for many reasons. One of the primary elements is grounding. These are times for dropping into ourselves, dropping into the earth and finding the substance of who we are. We sing and dance, read poetry, speak of our challenges. We set free—paradoxically taking in and learning from—that which does not serve, and bind ourselves to the importance of our being, the beauty and danger of manifested flesh and blood, the immortal soul and all its ancestry. We find together, as in most kinds of community rituals, the very nectar of life's greatest gifts.

At these gatherings, men create homes—places both tangible and real—in their psyches where they can find their grounded worthiness. I say create because in many ways adults must choose their ways of being, their attitudes and how they want to enfold, both within and without. It is also true that we inherit certain propensities and soul work from our ancestors, that we can't choose to accept or abandon, but rather, must embrace. This is the role of the living, to some extent, to help heal the wounds of the ancestors. Still, there are many ways in which we can serve the inner and outer dimensions, many ways to prepare and to have healthy spaces for the expression of who we are.

The coming together itself provides what is needed. Many times, as we introduce ourselves in the beginning, men say they don't know why they're there, but they are glad to have come. They seem to feel themselves on the shores of a lake with brothers who understand, have been there too and may be there again. We don't necessarily have an outline of what is to happen. What needs to happen goes on in the spirit realm. Just showing up is enough to receive it.

Some of the men show up confused, worried, frightened at various crossroads in our lives. It is natural and initiatory to be uncertain, so long as there is a return, to what has meaning and sustains our souls. What we see today, it seems, is a spiraling outward, at greater velocities, with little return or replenishing. Much of our culture is entranced by the boom mentality—gather, gather, gather, and isolate in the treasures infused with mass media images of how wonderful it all is.

Humanity is no stranger to struggle. We come into times of chaos and are asked to look at our choices and bind to that which will sustain and enrich our existence. We come through the times of chaos, like the Dark Ages, and return again to the ways that allow us to thrive, further mature in the beauty of spiritual and natural forces, and find love at the center. In the refrain of Mozart: "Love, love, love, that is the soul of genius."

I sometimes look around at the accelerating population growth, the technological and economic growth, and wonder what it has accomplished. Has love been considered in the equation? Has there been an inherent appreciation for the fundamental spiritual needs of the people to be in nature, in prayer and community? Or have we instead separated ourselves from the children to maintain certain material standards? Have we left fathers and mothers with so little time and energy the best they can do is check out and hope nobody gets hurt? It seems to me the break has now grown wide enough that people can't help but notice. When high school assassins gun down twenty of their classmates and teachers, we begin to wake up. I see increasing evidence of a grassroots movement to bring people back together to reclaim community, the joy and struggle of living together and choosing a future with promise. People see that human encroachment on the natural world has to be limited—and they are doing something about it. They are stepping out of the nuclear family into second and third circle families where they can contribute to a larger vision. And so amidst the chaos and seeming totality of popular culture, a continual blooming of vital alternatives takes place. I am reminded of Walt Whitman's words:

There was never any more inception than there is now,
Nor any more youth or age than there is now;
And will never be any more perfection than there is now,
Nor any more heaven or hell than there is now.

All truths wait in all things,
They neither hasten their own delivery nor resist it,
They do not need the obstetric forceps of the surgeon,
The insignificant is as big to me as any,
What is less or more than a touch?

Logic and sermons never convince,
The damp of the night drives deeper into my soul.

All forces have been steadily employed to complete and delight me
Now I stand on this spot with my soul.

Do I contradict myself?
very well then… I contradict myself,
I am large…I contain multitudes.

I bequeath myself to the dirt to grow from the grass I love,
If you want me again look under your bootsoles
You will hardly know who I am or what I mean,
But I shall be good health to you nevertheless,
and filter and fiber your blood.
Failing to fetch me at first keep encouraged,
missing me one place search for another,
I stop somewhere waiting for you. [38]

I like the expansiveness of Walt Whitman's poem. It welcomes the many, the diverse. It also reminds us that there is no future utopia with more potential and capacity than we have now. Furthermore, it says we are not living in the worst of times either, but as usual for humanity, somewhere in between. No matter how crazy things appear, the natural act of caring lives in all circles. Thus the ancient blood of humanity vibrates within us to a sympathetic beat, the resonance of compassion that allows us to consider even the suffering of our enemies, that carves out a space for mercy in our hearts, even toward family members we love but have difficulty tolerating. The worst of violence, abuse, cruelty can take place in a family and yet the caring returns. In humble simple ways, the acknowledged man seeks reconciliation, often without saying anything, but through voluntary humility. Sometimes direct responsibility is claimed, but often not, and caring comes back anyway. When a conscious mending takes place everyone gets a bit of healing and the community of family gets stronger and kinder. In men's circles we call this the soul's work. These are the ways of growing and maintaining soul—by engaging in the moments of life. Here we can find our worthiness and our fullness. I don't mean to insinuate it is easy. Often we struggle to connect with others, but if we remain clear in our choice for healing and vision, things usually work out.

So often a veil or a wedge appears that drives us away from the necessary slowing and introspection of soul work. Call it what you will, name it, see it, question the demands of the modern world, a world that sees it as foolish or weak to be doing "God's work" in the world. Perhaps our ways of commerce and entertainment are enemies to soul and deep meaning. If so, they are the dark angels that make us strong, that challenge us and require a continual renewing of our dedication. When I'm working with youth I ask the question, "How do you stay connected to your heart and soul?" I ask, "To what spiritual force inside, what god or goddess, what spiritual team do you connect so that you live your life in the world of heart and soul?" These are the intersections of contemplation that are helpful if we can be open to them. In the bosom of rich questions our commitments are sustained.

The elders and the men have been my guides. What I have learned often came during the gatherings and Soul Retreats you've heard me mention. Usually we begin on Friday evening, camped out or at a retreat center of some kind. We begin in a large circle, often with a modest fire burning orange hot in the center. Men of all ages sit together. I cherish the opportunities I've had to join in such gatherings. At our opening circles, we call out our names and are welcomed by the circle. Each of us speaks briefly about the call or interest in coming to the camp. All forms of expression are welcome, silence included. Letting stillness speak often penetrates the most profoundly.

Depending on the wishes of the men present, there is often a soft background rhythm, drum, rattle, clap sticks or flute, which helps us to loosen up and be free of the usual mechanical rhythms. Music or percussion provides what we refer to as a sound field and allows our bodies to let go of their tight grip on life—the "fast lane" demands, family difficulties or a death still fresh. Room can be made for celebration, silly boy play and unlimited other possibilities. When we release our controlling grip on life, it puts us in a more natural relationship with the world that does not wish to be controlled by us. As Gabriel Garcia Marquez[39] says, "Nobody teaches life anything." It's an interesting process to witness these circles of men releasing their grips. I can almost hear jets of steam escaping as the grips let go, the great cracking and breaking up of winter's ice along a shoreline of the psyche.

Then we are open to the deeper reasons for our gatherings: to meet in mind and body at a slower pace, more aware of the moments. This slower atunement is actually closer to what our bodies know as the "normal world." It will catch up with us when we let go, drop into the pace of our heartbeat and breath. A simple healing takes place by the act of convergence between mind, body and spirit.

Further healing naturally follows. For some men, the convergence provides an outlet to grief. So often in our lives there isn't time or room for the grief that is so much a part of being an adult—watching grandparents and parents grow old and die, our friends come down with cancers and have heart attacks. It should come as no surprise that grief is often the gateway to healing. It is a gateway that naturally opens. It does not need to be coerced, tricked, or forced open, but comes on its own, at the proper time for each man, through the unspectacular practice of slowing down and coming into sync with our natural rhythms.

I speak about this right away: the gathering is not meant to be anything greatly magical, mind-blowing or impressive. Maybe one day we will even hold a sweat purification ceremony without the hot rocks. We will find enough inspiration together without having a dramatic rush of heat and steam. It may be possible it is enough that we are together, engaged in union with the beauty of man's nature with the beauty of earth nature. We gather to drink from the well of our ancestral wisdom that is seated in the care of all people. Any healing, blessing or vision that comes from the collective of men—whatever the means, be it ritual, dancing, story telling, solo time—comes out of our basic orientation to natural beauty and the wisdom of the ancestors. Those of us who are called to guide such camps make an effort to serve the container, to be present with as much integrity as possible, so that all the participants may find our life ways.

We go through a weekend together, helping each other guide the experience. We create rituals, spaces or containers for specific prayers. We create altars sometimes to symbolize a specific world issue or a common theme among those gathered. During the Gulf War, for example, we created an altar and conducted a vigil for three days and nights, with a soft drum going the whole time. We do whatever it takes, whatever is possible, to serve healing and empowerment. Our dedication is to the soul work of those present, the magnum opus that is their lives. We help each other sometimes by not helping—letting a man roll in the mud with his demons and simply witnessing him consciously and compassionately. We hold the container and trust ourselves, our own intuition, spirit teams and ancestors to guide us.

Frequently young men are drawn to the camps by their fathers or uncles. Their intuition, so often cut off from their intellects, has somehow guided them to take the risk and accept the invitation. At a certain point during the gatherings the young men are brought forward, often painted with colors that represent the four directions of the earth. An old grandfather's hunting knife, preserved and honored over the years, is scraped across their bodies, in a symbolic gesture that says all life takes life, that destruction or creation are equal possibilities. We challenge the young men to take responsibility for these powers within themselves.

We counsel with them backed up to a fire, so the heat of their life and the question of who they are to become cannot drain away. The fire's touch pushes it back in on them. The elders speak, not to give advice, but in support of the young man's importance in the world and his worthiness to receive the gifts of an initiated adult life.

The young men stand with fire in front and fire behind. For most of them it is a difficult scene to trust, and yet the power of thirty men holding them in a pensive awareness is usually enough to melt their mistrust. By getting partially cooked, sweating, being seen, under the uncertain future of a sharp hunting knife, they connect to an awareness of just what is happening, why it is required, and what is to be gained by going through it.

I do not consider these full and traditional initiations. The word "initiation" is used in excess these days. I consider these "markings" and often refer to them as a "welcoming," part of a man's initiation that continues throughout his life. A friend of mine was told by an Australian Aboriginal elder the four main virtues of an initiated man. The elder said, "He has to have a song, a dance, a dream, and a story."

When the ritual is complete, the young men are asked to take their place among the older men. They join the circle with a new understanding of what growing up means. The men who witness are also bathed in the truth of spirit set free in a young man's world. They sometimes feel sadness, recalling their own youth, and the lack of such rituals to help them cross into manhood. All of us know, without having to speak it directly, something important has taken place.

Who is this for? Who comes? Men of all conditions, all ages. A man does not have to be broken in spirit to attend a Spirit Camp. Participation, as I see it, is more aligned with the ancient spiritual traditions from around the world. It is normal and common in the old ways to gather with brothers and place one's life journey in a sacred container, to be considered, laughed at and redirected. It was not something special that only an elite few did. In fact, it was no more extraordinary than gathering water or weaving a basket. It was and is the service each person provides to the community and the natural world, which is one and the same.

At our gatherings, after each of us has begun to find our personal ground, we call in the teaching energies, the helping souls of our ancestors, the cardinal directions, east, south, west, north, above, below, and center. The directional energies are in themselves powerful guides to life's passages and wisdom. We call in, directly, the spirits and helping allies in this life journey. For some men, this is a difficult process. Often, we do not have a feeling of connection to our lineage. Our resistance is an appeal to our ancestors and this resistance becomes our medicine.

Many have had no experience of being supported, by others or by Spirit. It is hard for them to imagine a team of spirit guides, ready to help, assist, teach and serve. So often such assistance is subtle, and the senses for perceiving it have atrophied. For many, the camp is a form of knocking on the inner doors and awakening former ways of knowing. It doesn't happen all at once, but it isn't unusual for men who were completely shut down to such possibilities to open to them in short periods of time.

After the first night, quite often filled with prophetic dreams, men are awakened by soft music. They enter a day filled with soul work through councils, ritual creations, dance, solitude, story telling, the art of deep listening, meditation, singing, prayer, and more than anything, laughter. Laughter plays an important role in cooling off the intensity that builds up from the attention and focusing. Humor is critical in the mix or any soul work, any ritual. Each man comes into his four directions in his own way, as his own adult guide, his own person capable of blessing others and being blessed. He challenges himself to grow into the service of his life and to give his gifts. He also challenges his brothers to grow, to give their gifts, find their meaning and purpose and give them to their people... all people.

The camps are not easy. Tempers flair. We get into conflicts. We do radical ritual and it isn't about making life nice. It is about following the soul inside, tasting the spirit of evolution, of healing and faith, linking it into the body as a physical, biological experience. As Meister Eckhart has said, "The soul loves the body." Thus it is essential that our work be grounded in the body, made physical, felt in the nerves, the organs, the cells, for the soul is the body, the blood its rivers, as it is for the whole of nature and humanity.

I have been guiding these retreats for fifteen years. It never fails that Spirit, our ancestors and the physical place help and guide and nurture the men who are there. Some do not feel this, cannot receive the blessing, and do not receive a gut connection. This is a sign that other ways or other containers await these men. To paraphrase Rumi, There are "a hundred ways to kneel and kiss the earth," to love the I and thus the other.

In the end of our ordinary dream time together we give thanks for our allies, helpers, ancestors, the place, each other. We release the call for support of the four directions, and the above and below, with gratitude. We are reminded that we take all the blessings and allies with us into our daily lives. We remember that we are connected always to the spirit allies and our ancestral world. We discuss incorporation, the dangers in the world we return to, the grip that will want to grab onto our usual struggles. And we remember, as Stephen Foster and Meredith Little say, "The world we return to is not only profane, but equally sacred."

With this in mind we consider the communities to which we return. They are waiting for us to care for them, to support, enhance and foster them. We release the energies gathered for the camp and venture out, nourished, more grounded and replenished. As we release our helping spirits, we speak our thanks for their help in making our rituals strong. We thank them for their inspiration, the way they've nourished our souls and thus our communities. We verbally release the allies, because the act of praying out loud reaches the essence of our bodies. Our flesh knows and trusts the spoken word, and when we hear ourselves and others speak it is believable to the psyche.

The challenge for modern man, it seems to me, is to believe in himself, to have faith that no matter his occupation, his status or his history, he is an *important* part of human evolution. Our culture is so dominated by issues of work and material status that many, many men feel powerless and are unable to be meaningful healing forces in society. Many men give up on life because they do not measure up to the commercial standards set forth as the judges of virtue. I say these are false myths of what it is to be a man. Life is not a competition based on who can acquire the most amounts or greatest size. This is a hike down a dead-end road. How many men do you know who have spent their lives attempting to acquire enough material possessions to soothe a longing that really exists in their hearts and souls? The ancestors, the soul, the way of life that brings healing, that brings joy, has little relation to the stock market, our cars or the size of our houses. True security lies in the valley of the human heart, in how one is loving his people, and is being loved. These are the treasures of a rich man.

Normal day, let me be aware of the treasures you are. Let me learn
from you, savor you, bless you before you depart. Let me not pass
you by in quest of some rare and perfect tomorrow. Let me hold
you while I may, for it will not always be so. One day, I shall dig my
nails into the earth, or bury my face in the pillow, or stretch myself
taut, or raise my hands to the sky, and want, more than all the
world, your return.   —Mary Jean Irwin[40]

THE INQUIRY INTO SIMPLICITY IS AMONG THE GREAT HOLY QUESTIONS
that has been with humanity forever. It brings us to a central paradox:
the very contemplation of simplicity draws us into complexity. The idea
of living in uncluttered ways, with hearts connected to the undying
truths that sustain the joy of life, can quickly become complicated.
Once our brains get a hold of the concept, they can systematically lead
us into a labyrinth and we may find ourselves yearning for those simpler
times when we didn't worry about simplicity. Add to that a plethora of
cultural judgments that associate simplicity, or simple living, with apathy, a lack of ambition, even stupidity. We are generally groomed for the
showy and impressive life, loaded with material wealth, driving ambition, electronic day timers, cellular phones, pagers, career and social
demands that tell the world we're busy and "making it." The old ways
of seeking council with the elders and tending to the children can't compete. They lack pizzazz. Simple spiritual practices, such as quiet prayers,
solitary contemplation, walks in nature, finding inclusiveness for all
deities and gods, are often looked upon as shallow, uneducated, even
heathenish.

Behind these judgments, however, I sense an often overlooked
yearning. It is no surprise to me there is a large movement in America
today toward the question and pursuit of simplified living. Books have

been written and magazines created to help people recognize the difference between what they truly need and what they want. Simplicity is a way of making choices, of sorting out desires, of looking beneath the surface to what is truly calling to us. What so many of the men I've worked with find beneath the craving for some object is a primary desire for internal unity—a sense of peace, no matter what external life looks like. What they desire is a simple sense of purpose. They want to see themselves in some essential state, unmixed with the cluttered complexities that overwhelm them. They want to step out of the image-based marketplace and all of its demands: its excessive cunning, its requirements of wit, shadowy aggressiveness and immediate results. They want to find places where their simple natures are not bullied, where they can let the quiet prayers of their inner realm be heard. So many men want to lay down arms, stop attacking and defending, and slow down enough to make choices about how they use their precious life energy.

Often, along the way to simplicity we are asked to let go our attachments. The self-centered ways of control and power seem to push simplicity away. Simple men are often those who are less attached to their personal identity and more connected to a deeper collective wisdom. Simple men I've known let themselves be creative, often in small ways, with art, community service work, chores and small construction projects. These men are found in the soul's valley, where there is compassion toward all ways of evolution. Simple men do not lead boring lives. They do, in fact, quite regularly venture near the heart of chaos that lives at the quiet center. They touch the creative force that is the basis of life. They welcome unknown outcomes, mystery and serendipity.

What joyous confusion to know the simple truth of chaos. How grandly ridiculous to lean into the feeling of blind and blissful terror. Life, yes, and what of it? Chaos… the mixture of physical, mental, mystical infinity, constantly pouring into the natural world and asking us to play ball. The only guarantee is that chaos will be constant. Running through its nucleus we find simplicity. Simplicity in emotions, in visions, in choices, in grief, in sex, in death. Simplicity is the inherent necessity to sort out unruly chaos and render it into wisdom so that it may serve the people. To put order into life, even in fleeting moments, is what gives simplicity its royal position. The function of kings and queens is to reduce the chaos of chaos, help us find order and purpose.

Chaos and simplicity need each other. The very nature of birth, life, vision, healing and death brings these two together as one of nature's great dynamics. It appears, however, that in our times chaos is elevated to heroic status, while simplicity is synonymous with failure, as if a hallmark of the unmotivated slacker. Is it possible for contemporary man to reap the grace of a unity with life so deep that chaos becomes informative to human evolution rather than a dominant, self-defeating force of worldly destruction? Can we find ways to practice uniting chaos with simplicity, bringing the inner and outer worlds together in the dance? This is where the true greatness of life resides, in the unity of these apparent opposites. Somewhere in it is the humility to recognize a greatness beyond ourselves. Call it God, the divine or some absolute force. Whatever the name, a certain maturity comes to bear in the sacrifice of personal grandiosity. To unite with and be infused with the great mystery one cannot stand entirely apart. In some way a room must be built in the psyche that can contain a cauldron which renders chaos into simple truths. Often the simple truths connect to collective wisdom, filled with the learning of our million years experience in matters of the soul.

Without this space in the psyche it is difficult to find relief from the devouring voices coming at us in all forms of media, and from within as well. We live in chaotic times. Maybe it has always seemed this way throughout our history. What is new relates to sheer magnitude. There are six billion of us now. The explosion of people has happened like an algae bloom, most of it coming in the last hundred years. Our technologies link us, but to what? An image of material success that only brings more chaos, more destruction? So many of us are running hell bent downhill without brakes to the forefront of humanity's basic struggle—survival. A complex logical intelligence demands we serve only it, and we are enraged by its tyranny, unsatisfied by what it leaves behind.

Simplicity stands on the sidelines, holding an olive branch, a cup of cool water, a frond of palm to fan us. It waits for anyone who can slow down long enough to reach out and accept what there is to behold. As a spiritual practice it slowly and naturally renders down the maddening pace of life to a potential healing essence. That is why we hear elders who seek truth speak to us of finding a prayer way, one simple practice, and sticking with it. Therein lies the deepening, the quiet hush of something important. In our practice we find our ground, our root, in the uncluttered slowness, the small regular steps of toning down the demands and choosing clearly which ones *really* need to be addressed. In simple practices we find the ballast to our yearnings, the fulcrum where we can balance ourselves within life's greatness and potential.

Simplicity, in contrast to the digital age, asks us to slow down and be aware of how we can be overwhelmed, and of how dangerous that can be. Simplicity asks us to reconsider the 5000 MHz processor and relate to the old learning that a scroll of parchment and a quill pen brought, to bring the spirit and the computer together. It asks us to sit by a stream and empty our minds as if they were tributaries. Simplicity does not, as some might think, demand that we give up the natural storms of intense feelings, passion or romance. What it does suggest is that we not sail rudderless in these turbulent waters. It cautions us to return to life's simple truths, compassion, meaning and inherited wisdom. To not revisit a sense of life's enjoyment is to remain in a never ending storm, a prison of chaos and struggle, absent grace, peace, calm and gentility. What sailor does not appreciate the teachings of the storm all the more after anchoring in a safe harbor and sharing the tale with friends at a warm inn?

This is the story of becoming who we are born to be. Its structure is found in the simple witnessing of what unites us with the wonder and beauty of all life. Margaret Mead speaks of such discovery in her famous quote:

> Never doubt that a small group of people can change the world. For it has always been true that it was small groups who have changed the world.[41]

In these words is a simple truth, an endorsement of—for lack of better words—what might be called smallness, its power to affect change and bring benefits. Margaret Mead's words speak to a yearning inside the body, seemingly small and simple, and yet capable of changing the world from the inside out.

The act of prayer is one way to open the ground of human soul for such potential. Along the way of a regular practice, the seeds of a new life, healing and unity with evolution can find fertile ground. These seeds may have to pass through our outward-oriented culture and its prejudices against the search for a simple existence and the meaning found in such a path. It is worth the effort to pass through our exterior constructs. Though they represent a genuine need for safety and protection, ironically they produce the opposite: nervousness, discomfort and emptiness, regardless of how rapidly the investment portfolio expands. More stability and peace exists in letting go of our exterior constructs and returning to the cycles of life that hold the core values we have known for a long time. Our forebears sculpted the shapes of these values as guides to the inner wilderness. They are waiting to share them with us. Also available, and necessary, is the coaching and support of deep friendships, allies who can touch in with us as we move through life's challenges and cycles. Again it comes to slowing down. As in the spinning of a wheel, the outer edge moves at a dizzying speed. The more we can move to the interior, the easier it is to find our balance, until we reach the stillness of the center. From this vantage we can recognize how the constant grind on the spinning rim can make life spiritless and mechanical. How could it not require grasping and groping, out there on the cutting edge, feeling as if at any moment the centrifugal force will cast us into oblivion? It is natural to seek a move toward the center, and yet we usually deny ourselves such repose.

Through a regular simple practice, such as prayer, walking meditation or any number of the infinite ways one can feel connected, we allow ourselves to find the slowness of center. Moments of awareness flood us with meaning. We see unusual colors—ones that don't even exist in the visible spectrum. Something like God, or a clearer awareness, appears in the greatness of natural beauty. This is not unusual, not supernatural or metaphysical. It is seen and known in the self not separated, the self joined to its center. Such a joining asks us to let go of the myth of protection in a fortress of amassed possessions. Sam Keene[42] has called it trapeze work, the art of letting go of one rung before having the next in one's grasp.

The stories I have heard about faith have taught me that faith, as a guiding force, does not happen instantaneously, nor can it be held onto once discovered. It can be built through a simple step-by-step practice of awareness, paying attention to the weave of inner truth and outer circumstance. Here we find the movement of polarities, the exchange, as I related earlier, between chaos and simplicity. Once we can notice the paradox without having to figure it out, there exists the possibility Walt Whitman discovered of living in the largeness of our contradictions. Lo and behold, grace. Value felt in the body, not ethereal but concrete, comes to us when we allow the moment (wherever we find ourselves now), to touch us and communicate with us deeply. The world offers its beauty constantly in subtle ways, yet so often it is passed by. The other day at a restaurant I noticed a little boy, his aliveness receptive to kindness between two souls, attention, a blessing perhaps. I smiled at him and walked by, feeling in the moment something shift, slip, an opportunity lost. I walked by, passing up an opportunity to see his beauty fully in the moment. In the practice of wakefulness such opportunities are recognized—and they are abundant. We talk in these times of wanting abundance in our lives. For the man who slows down, it becomes abundantly clear how truly rich are the waters in which we swim. Like the fat trout, tuned in and focused, he sees a thousand juicy morsels float by in a continual stream.

Perhaps our culture would punish a man lounging like a lazy trout in the current. Perhaps he would be passed over for promotion or let go in a re-engineering scheme. He may appear to lack dedication. And yet I ask, what possible salary, bonus or pension plan could possibly compare to the profound and deeply life-changing experience of opening his heart and reaching out for grace? Is there any beauty more compelling than the simple wisdom of an awake soul, touching and knowing life through the intelligence of the heart?

One of the ways I notice men touching these places is through a life bound to chores, the simple tended to what needs to be done. Some are poetry. I notice men attending town meetings to help their communities grow in healthy ways. These men make an investment in their chores. Through them whole realms of awareness spring forth. Their conscious attention to the environment becomes the gateway for new perceptions. Time is the investment, as is always the case. What we value, we give our time to, and what we give our time to provides us with rewards. Chores give back something subtle, honest and palpable. It could be called meaning. The cut wood asks to be split. There is meaning in what Thoreau calls being warmed twice: once in the chopping and again in the burning. There is a back and forth reciprocity.

Mankind grew up through a practice of holy chores. For most of us, this has been replaced, by-and-large, with excessive shopping. To market to market to buy a fat pig, home again home again jigity jig… and what we leave behind is a tragic loss. The self is cheated out of meaningful engagement with real tasks of survival. Chores are sacrificed to a path so dangerous many of us get lost on it our entire lives. The lucky ones, in my judgment, get thrown off the merry-go-round. Something slows them down: the birth of a child, an unexpected illness, the sudden end to a career—by choice or otherwise. In this slower reality, they may find themselves suddenly intrigued with the possibility of dry walling the basement.

There's something about being aligned with a few basic heart and soul truths that brings us to the great mystery, to great depth and direction. It doesn't surprise me that something so basic as gathering eggs from the hen house would bring one to the epic question of all time: Why am I here? It is a question that, to me, resembles the cud of a cow. It does not have an answer. It cannot be solved only by the mind. And yet, chewing on it somehow satisfies. Great revelations that stun the vocal chords to stillness come out of the simple spiritual yearning for purpose. Fruits of magical tenderness and sweet juiciness ripen when a man or woman steps away from the clutter, drops metaphysical contrivances, the countless concerns of a busy life, and chews the cud of eternal inquiry.

In our men's gatherings over the last fifteen years a truth has emerged along these lines. The bounty of a simple life does not come without effort. Clear and fortified intention, a strong and ever replenished commitment, and for some a daily physical and spiritual practice are necessary to follow one's vision and heart. The practice is to keep our eyes open, especially to the current world energy that is often not in support of inner bushwhacking. I'm not saying modern times are all wrong or a bad thing. However, the temptation and seduction to diminish oneself *does exist* and has a very real inertia with which we must contend. Once a man commits, he is set free and united with his potential, his holy journey and the simple awareness of choice. Compassion erupts from his soul as it vibrates to the ancient chords of meaning. The Goethe poem included earlier expresses it as well as anything.

In Jacob Needleman's book, *Money and the Meaning of Life*,[43] he speaks of being able to "discriminate the eternal [human truths] from the transitory in yourself." This is the sort of contemplation that leads to inner dialogue, a sensitivity to the voices of self, each deserving respect. In a process so directed, a quality of discernment emerges that can dissolve away much of the transitory values and attitudes that keep many a man broken. It is only natural that a question of value would ask us to examine our relationship to the current cultural values of success and entangling complexities, relative to the inherent benefits of a simple life. A man cannot slow down to the pace of inquiry without recognizing how the external spinning can deny him the subtle inner world of growth and healing. In the modality of simplicity the beauty and brilliance of life thrives in unsuspected ways. With a few basic truths to reflect on during our daily travels, we are fueled in our worthiness and can see the meaning in family, community and livelihood. Simplicity relates to a sense of moment-to-moment wonder. Many a busy hardworking man or woman do live simple lives through the graces found in what Mary Jean Irwin calls a "normal day." She reminds us, "Let me not pass you by in quest of some rare and perfect tomorrow."

Along the way, a basic form of release and regeneration comes back to us time and time again. Simple rest. So many of the men I encounter are dog tired, but they have forgotten how to rest. Perhaps more accurately, they don't feel they have permission to rest. The dictate of constant doing and being done to pulls men out of themselves, makes it impossible for them to be satisfied. If there is anything that makes us more agitated and angry than this constant pressure, please let me know. I have noticed in myself what happens when I stay too long on the hard spinning exterior. When a man forgets to rest, his heart and feelings go into a recessed cage. A certain pointedness comes into his bearing. I become unable to notice the subtle offerings of beauty that pass by me at every moment. It is so easy, so seductive, this maelstrom of commercialism that calls on me to try harder, to rarely be satisfied or at peace. I wouldn't be expressing any great revelation to speak of the loss of personal time over the last hundred years. In the past, the religious traditions recognized the importance of regenerative and reflective spaces in life. The Sabbath, for example, represents one of our traditions in the West. We knew—and still know behind the facade—that people simply do not do well without rest. We need to relax, to play and deeply celebrate the wonder of life. Do you ever find yourself in a shopping mall, an airport, on a city street downtown, and you look at yourself and realize you're not there? You're off in another world, thinking about yesterday, tomorrow, or what might happen if...? And you look around at the other people, who seem also to be absent, off on some dream journey. Few notice or acknowledge each other. Many of the faces appear enormously tired, wanting more than anything a day of rest. All of us running, running, way ahead of ourselves, *ahead of our souls.*

The soul moves slowly. It appreciates the joy of rest and makes it a priority. In these fast-paced times, the soul seems something of a shadow. It lags back a few steps from the body of a man or woman rushing to the next appointment. It goes along as a niggling anchor, a subtle friction, and waits for a chance, maybe, for the man or woman to let it catch up with them and show them their meaning and purpose.

I can recall growing up in a culture that never spoke of rest. The only place I witnessed a slower pace was with my grandparents, who finally, after a lifetime of incessant labor, allowed themselves to slow down and relax. I was so drawn to them as a boy and young man. They had something that was missing. I didn't know what it was at the time, but my soul brought me to the elders whenever it could. With them I could catch up with myself in ways that weren't allowed out there, where godliness lived in the exchange of goods and services. In the presence of my grandparents I picked up pieces of truth in the tattered edges of worn carpets. I found the richness of rest, renewal, letting go of responsibility and control.

In my years of working with men, I have heard others recall similar attractions to elders or the pace of nature. They tell these stories, sometimes with guilt, as if it was wrong for them to take these liberties, even in youth. To consider stopping as adults, simplifying or resting, terrifies so many men. They say, "The whole damn thing would fall apart!" Men have literally told me they think they would die if they slowed down. If they were to relax, technology would pass them by, they would become obsolete and be discarded. In the safe container of a soulful council, these men regularly come to the realization they are defeated anyway. They are burnt out shells of their god-given beauty, half dead from hurrying to keep up. They realize they are slaves to an inhuman pace, to a machine pace, a computer pace. They have given up rest, given up their loves, sacrificed their bliss for the promised spoils of victory. When they realize how complete their defeat, up bubbles the grief.

What profound sadness to be hit with a bankrupt pattern of dominance and violence, family breakdown, the search for relief through entertainment, only to find more loneliness. In illusion we often find only more illusion. I wonder, do you have the tools with which to question the choices you make? Are you able to step back and examine your life with any objectivity? The mind as an organ of outward perception loves illusion. We are driven by these illusions. Do they embody eternal truths, or are they as likely to evaporate as a mist in the sun? When we bind ourselves to illusions, we evaporate right along with them. Rest is the way to release our grip on emptiness. It is the way of return, to the infinite riches of the inner world, where our bodies can receive the world's blessing.

Many say the task of modern man is to reorient ourselves to the inward journey. In so doing, we may then return to the external material world and temper it with the substance of eternal value, as Needleman says. This is our dilemma: to live as we do in the daily necessities of survival, the need to breathe, drink, eat, be sheltered, rest, while also living in the lifelong question of what is eternal and how to remain awake to its force in our lives. This is where it gets interesting.

The men I've come to know who are engaged in the work of meaning and prayer have shown me glimpses of what is eternal in the soul of humanity. Almost all of them have discovered their own unique ways into the story of eternal blessedness. They have come in contact with an innate desire to know themselves and bring forth their ability to enact change and bring atonement into their communities. Some men focus on their families, refine their ability to be kind and generative husbands and fathers. Often they branch out from there and extend their blessings to the youth in their communities. Others find expression in art. They write poems, carve wood, paint, make music, and offer these to the people. In many cases, they don't make a dime from these efforts. They volunteer because it feeds their hearts, and this exchange links them with the eternal, the simple. Many of these soul men actively preserve nature and may dedicate themselves to keeping watersheds, air and land healthy. They recognize their connection with earth, the four seasons and the harmony among all the elements.

Usually they come to appreciate the forces of opposition, that live in themselves and in the world. They bless the resistance and give thanks for something to push up against. They do not, however, accept the precepts of the way it has to be—the way that seems to cut humanity off from its natural connection to life. These men have standards. They practice what is right and true for themselves without blame or judgment.

Long before I found myself guided into this work, I noticed an interest in the meaning of life among men, women, elders and youth who were living through life's forces and giving their gifts to the world. As a young man I was not able to feel the truth and power of this kind of love. I did not recognize it as a core truth that runs through the blood of all humans. My youthful troubles, my own inflations and arrogance, kept me at bay from the gifts of life. Still, my deeper, less linear self received the blessing of these elders and peers seeking meaning. Nature also played a key role in sending me the message that my life had a purpose, that I was not a mistake, and my existence was important. My unconscious stored it for later, as a chipmunk would cache plump seeds. In time it began to dawn on me that something critical was missing in my life. I began to look for what that was, and stumbled upon the cache of seeds from my elders. Luckily, my blood had stayed warm enough to carry the old messages up to consciousness. Thanks to my ancestors, and their diligent effort to keep their blood warm and keep the messages alive, I had the capacity to hear what had been said. I was able to break through the hardened and selfish attitudes of an angry young man.

Slowly the layers of projection, inflation and prejudice toward anything different than myself began to soften and fall away. This process of owning my own projections—the way I think it should go—is an ongoing process. Through the relentless love of my parents, elders, teachers and nature I began to appreciate the ways of simplicity. I can remember clearly one of the softening times. I had blown my knee out playing college football. It was the end of my gridiron career. I felt lost, alone, my life without meaning. I went to the icy shores of Lake Superior in the upper peninsula of Michigan and stood in the power and solitude of that place, my leg in a cast, but really, my whole being in a cast. The wind on that frozen lake, the blowing snow, the rugged terrain, the ominous sky, all conspired to crack open my hardened exterior. When the cast over my being broke open in this mighty natural place, a deeper healing began to happen. The meaning of my life began to rise out of the dark struggles of my life. I entered the long slow process of healing and nurturing the wondrous gift that is my life.

I ask, when have you had painful blessings in your life? Have your people, the elders and nature touched you? Have you noticed the sparks of what is eternal at some time in your life? Have you known these feelings that tell you even the worst in life, the most difficult struggles, can be softened in a moment of peace? It is a simple exercise to go back into your experience, find the times of blessing, those people, the bridge that in some way invested you with a reflection of your own deep beauty. To acknowledge these blessings, the people and places, is to honor them, and yourself. Over the years certain people or times in nature come back to me again and again. It is important to acknowledge the memories and the souls that touched us in mysterious and wondrous ways that have lives of their own. I call it a blessing nectar, an essence of pure nourishment that existed long before me and will go on long after I am gone. In some way, it is man's charge in life—his responsibility to keep and care for this sweet nectar, for his own fulfillment and thus the world. As an elder of mine, Steven Foster, said to me, "You must slough off the garment of youthful freedom, and find that freedom in your dedication to family and community." Even when a man forgets his connection (most of us do now and then) the memory of being touched with the unifying force of purpose is never forgotten.

This returning is a basic practice of the simple life. And it is not easy. Unparalleled forms of contrivance vie for our attention. We live in an age of visual media capable of truly hypnotic creations. To stay awake is difficult, and yet, many do. I notice among those I admire, those who put themselves authentically behind their smiles, a certain vibration seems to emanate from a cellular level. These are frequently not people who live in isolation, cloistered away from the world. They are often very busy, but among their activities a sense about them is connected to life's simple and enduring truths. They seem to have an ability to see through the transitory deceptions of our current mythologies. They are not identified with greed, anger, the false god of money. At the same time they aren't poor or having to do without, for the most part. They are not, most of them, living in the country, chopping wood and carrying water. However, if the chance came along to do just that, most of them would take it.

What I'm trying to illustrate is what is possible. It is dangerous to live in a condition of perpetual bother, in which all attention is focused on what is wrong with the world. This is a habit that can lead only to unhappiness. What is wrong is not solved by our complaints about it. A deeply respected elder in our community, Airic Leonardson, Dancing Grandfather, is fond of quoting the *Tao Te Ching*, a book of Chinese truth similar to the *Bible* or the *Koran*. The passage goes something like this:

The dedicated student hears of Tao and practices it diligently.
The average student hears of it and considers it now and then.
The poor student hears of Tao and laughs out loud.
Without laughter, Tao would not be Tao.

Walt Whitman knows about this. He knows there will never be any more perfection than there is now. I don't always know this. I want to know and so I lean in that direction. J. Heider's book, *The Tao of Leadership*,[44] is a good reminder of the simple path. His rendering of the ancient Chinese sage, Lao Tzu, provides a wonderful contrast to models of control and aggression. It is a book filled with truths that endure through time.

Joseph Needleman says that "the problem with writing about life and living is that it makes it sound easy." I think he's right. Any message that comes to you with the promise of easy satisfaction is suspect. That is why it is healthy, as the bumper sticker advises us, to question authority. Question the predominant messages about what constitutes success, what brings happiness. Are the people you know who have given themselves completely to the mechanics of commercial enterprise happy? What has been given up in such service? It's not necessary to scorn or vilify the ways of popular culture. It is, however, important to question its direction.

I have witnessed many fulfilling alternatives to the status quo. They have given me serious reservations about the modern way of life that can rob us of simple joys. Too often I have heard those trapped on the treadmill speak of their misery. They know the golden apple is not growing there, but they do not know how to get off and travel another road. Who needs convincing of this in the presence of so many broken homes, so much environmental devastation, so many senseless acts of violence? Anyone who reads a paper or watches the news can't help but be troubled by the trends.

It is about commiserating, the practice of melding the paradoxes and the growing challenges that we all must face. Many people in the world have been in the strong flow of spiritual evolution before us. What interests me are the individual choices to be different. I'm attracted to those who make a statement by the way they live their lives. It takes a clear, organic and flexible *intention*, a strong commitment, healthy discipline, much practice, attention to one's heart and soul questions, a willingness to re-evaluate. This is the path that holds promise of an evolving future for humanity. I am grateful for the gifts of the contemporary life. I salute the simple ways, and encourage anyone who is the least bit attracted to this magic that lies within to continue and to begin the journey again and always. "To leap into the poetry of life," as the great poet Robert Bly says. It is the jumping into one's great heart and soul, continuing what began millions of years ago with beneficial fortune that allows a freshness to be found. As it is high atop the tundra above tree line, our lives turn with each passing season. We mirror the earth, moving from birth to youth, adult and elder unto death. Let us begin. Let us continue.

End Notes

1. Oliver, Mary. *New And Selected Poems* (Boston, Beacon Press, 1992).

2. Rilke, Rainer Marie. *Letters to a Young Poet* (New York, W.W. Norton & Company Inc., 1934).

3. Frankl, Viktor E. *Man's Search for Meaning* (New York, Pocket Books, 1959, 1963).

4. Thomas, Lewis. *The Lives of a Cell: Notes of a Biology Watcher* (New York, Bantam Books, 1974).

5. Mails, Thomas E. *Fools Crow* (Lincoln, Bison Book, 1979, 1990).

6. Dossey, Larry, M.D. *Healing Words, The Power Of Prayer And The Practice Of Medicine* (New York, HarperCollins, 1993).

7. Van der Post, Laurens. *The Heart of the Hunter: Customs and Myths of the African Bushman* (San Diego, Harcourt Brace Jovanovich, 1961).

8. Thoreau, Henry David. *Walden* (New York, Signet Books, 1960).

9. Walker, Alice. *The Way Forward is With a Broken Heart* (New York, Random House, 2000).

10. Meade, Michael. *Men and the Water of Life: Intiation and the Tempering of Men* (San Francisco, HarperSanFrancisco, 1993).

11. Bly, Robert. *Selected Poems of Rainer Maria Rilke: A Translation from the German and Commentary* (New York, HarperCollins, 1981).

12. Hanh, Thich Nhat. *Call Me By My True Names: The Collected Poems of Thich Nhat Hanh* (Berkley, Parallax Press, 1999).

13. Whyte, David. *The Heart Aroused: Poetry and the Preservation of the Soul in Corporate America* (New York, Currency Doubleday, 1994).

14. DeMello, Anthony. *The Song Of The Bird* (New York, Double Day, 1984).

15. Golas, Thaddeus. *The Lazy Man's Guide to Enlightenment* (New York, Bantam Books, 1972).

16. Teish, Luisah. *Carnival of the Spirit: Seasonal Celebrations and Rites of Passage* (San Francisco, HarperSanFrancisco, 1994).

17. Myss, Carloyn and C., Norman, Shealy *Anatomy of the Spirit: The Seven Stages of Power and Healing* (New York, Random House, 1997).

18. Foster, Steven and Little, Meredith *The Four Shields: The Initiatory Seasons of Human Nature* (Big Pine, Lost Borders Press, 1998). *The Roaring Of The Sacred River: The Wilderness Quest for Vision and Self-Healing* (New York, Prentice Hall Press,1989).

19. Mindell, Arnold. *Sitting in the Fire: Large group transformations using conflict and diversity* (Portland, Lao Tse Press, 1995).

20. Stafford, William. *The Way It Is: New and Selected Poems* (Saint Paul, Greywolf Press, 1960, 1998).

21. Williamson, Marianne. *A Return To Love: Reflections on the Principles of A Course in Miracles* (New York, HarperCollins, 1992).

22. Johnson, Robert A. *Owning Your Own Shadow: Understanding The Dark Side Of The Psyche* (San Francisco, HarperSanFrancisco, 1991).

23. Bly, Robert. *A Little Book On The Human Shadow* (San Francisco, HarperSanFrancisco, 1988).

24. Rumi, Jelaluddin. *Essential Rumi: Translated by Coleman Barks* (Putney, Threshold Books, 1995).

25. Lawrence, D. H. *D. H. Lawrence: The Complete Poems* (New York, Penguin Books 1971).

26. Kessler, Rachael. *The Soul of Education: Helping Students Find Connection, Compassion and Character at School* (Alexandria, Association for Supervision and Curriculum Development, 2000).

27. Jastrab, Joseph. *Sacred Manhood Sacred Earth: A Vision Quest into the Wilderness of a Man's Heart* (New York, HarperCollins, 1994).

28. Lee, John. *Growing Yourself Back Up: Understanding Emotional Regression* (New York, Three Rivers Press, 2001).

29 Gurian, Michael. *The Good Son: Shaping The Moral Development Of Our Boys And Young Men* (New York, Jeremy P. Tarcher/Putnam, 1999).

30. Arrien, Angeles. *The Four-Fold Way: Walking the Paths of the Warrior, Teacher, Healer, and Visionary* (New York, HarperSanFrancisco, 1993).

31. March, Louise. *Gold Dust* (Middlesex, Rochester Folk Art, 1980).

32. Somé, Malidoma Patrice. *Of Water and the Spirit: Ritual, Magic, and Initiation in the Life of an African Shaman* (New York, Arkana Penguin Books, 1994).

33. Muller, Wayne. *How, Then, Shall We Live?: Four Simple Questions That Reveal the Beauty and Meaning of Our Lives* (New York, Batam Books, 1996).

34. Rumi, Jelaluddin. *Open Secret; Versions of Rumi: Translated by John Moyne and Coleman Barks* (Putney, Threshold Books, 1984).

35. Bly, Robert. *Selected Poems of Rainer Maria Rilke: A Translation from the German and Commentary* (New York, HarperCollins, 1981).

36. Campbell, Joseph. *The Hero With A Thousand Faces* (Princeton, Princeton University Press, 1949, 1968).

37. Trott, Susan. *The Holy Man* (New York, Riverhead Books, 1995)

38. Whitman, Walt. *Leaves Of Grass* (New York, The Modern Library, 1891-2)

39. Marquez, Gabriel Garcia. *Love In the Time of Cholera* (New York, Alfred A. Knopf, 1988).

40. Irwin, Mary Jean. *The Moon Is Not Enough* (Grand Rapids, Zondervan, 1978).

41. Mead, Margaret. *Blackberry Winter: My Earlier Years* (New York, Wm. Morrow & Co., 1972).

42. Keene, Sam. *Fire In The Belly: On Being A Man* (New York, Bantam Books, 1991).

43. Needleman, Jacob. *Money and the Meaning Of Life* (New York, Doubleday/Currency, 1991).

44. Heider, John. *The Tao of Leadership: Leadership Strategies for a New Age* (New York, Bantam Books, 1985).

Additional References

The Men's Council Project • Leadership Training Program
Heart and soul-based experiential trainings
Tom Daly, Jeffrey Duvall, Keith Fairmont
1955 Poplar Lane, Boulder, CO 80466
Phone and Fax: 303-444-9066
Email: menscouncil@aol.com

School Of Lost Borders • Lost Borders Press
Youth and adult rites of passage programs
P.O. Box 55, Big Pine, CA 93513
Email: lostbrds@tclis.org
Web site: www.schooloflostborders.com

Institute for Social and Emotional Learning
Rachael Kessler
3833 N. 57th Street, Boulder, CO 80301
Email: selrachael@aol.com

The Living Arts Foundation, Inc. • Four Quarters Coaching
Tom Daly PhD and Jude Blitz CHT
P.O. Box 17341, Boulder, Colorado 80301
Phone: 303-530-3337
Email: laffound@earthlink.net
Web site: www.livingartsfoundation.com

Shadow Work Seminars, Inc.
Cliff Barry and Mary Ellen Blandford
13076 Buckhorn Rd., Loveland, CO 80538
Phone: 970-203-0400
Email: shadowwk@frii.com
Web site: www.shadowwork.com,

Institute of Cultural Affairs
Youth rites of passage
Stan Crow
22421 39th Avenue SE, Bothell, WA 98021-7941
Phone: 425-486-5164
Email: icarlc@igc.org,
Web site: http://www.ICAjourneys.org/index.htm

Peer™ Training • The Detour Method
Healing rage, anger and regression
John Lee
201 Brentwood Court, Woodstock, GA 30188
Email: theflyingboy@aol.com
Web site: www.flyingboy.com

Further Reading

Snyder, Gary. *The Practice of the Wild* (San Francisco, North Point Press, 1990)

Bly, Robert. *The Sibling Society: An Impassioned Call For The Rediscovery Of Adulthood* (New York, Vintage Books, 1977).

Richo, David. *Shadow Dance: Liberating The Power & Creativity Of Your Dark Side* (Boston, Shambhala Publications, Inc., 1999).

Olds, Sharon. *The Father* (New York, Alfred A. Knopf, 1992).

Moore, Robert., Giillette, Douglas. *King Warrior Magician Lover: Rediscovering The Archetypes Of The Mature Masculine* (San Francisco, HarperSanFrancisco,1990).

Prechtel, Martin. *Secrets Of The Talking Jaguar: Memoirs From The Living Heart Of A Mayan Village* (New York, Jeremy P. Tarcher, 1998).

Adams, Cass. *The Soul Unearthed: Celebrating Wildness and Personal Renewal Through Nature* (New York, Tarcher/Putman, 1996).

Gurian, Michael. *Boys and Girls Learn Differently! (SanFrancisco, Jossey-Bass,* 2001).

Blake, William. *Songs Of Innocence and Of Experience: Showing the Two Contrary States of the Human Soul* (New York, Oxford University Press, 1967).

Gibran, Kahlil. *The Prophet* (New York, Alfred A Knopf, 1966).

Rumi, Jelaluddin. *Delicious Laughter: Rambunctious Teaching Stories from the Mathnawi* (Athens, Maypop Books,1990).

Kauth, Bill. *A Circle Of Men: The Original Manual For Men's Groups* (New York, St. Martin's Press, 1992).

Harding, Christopher. *Wingspan: Bold Visions In The Time Of Masculine Renewal* (New York, St Martin's Press, 1992)

Aaland, Mikkel. *Sweat: The Illistrated Story* (Santa Barbara, Capra Press, 1978).

Gerzon, Mark. *Listening To Midlife: Turning Your Crises Into A Quest* (Boston, Shambhala, 1996).

Roberts, Elizabeth and Elias Amidon. *Earth Prayers From Around The World, 365 Prayers, Poems, And Invocations For Honoring The Earth* (New York, HarperCollins, 1991).

Additional Copies

Interested in obtaining additional copies of this book for your friends?

Stories of Men, Meaning and Prayer

  1-9 copies $15 ea.

  10 copies or more $13 ea.

  25 copies or more $10 ea.

  Plus $2 per copy for postage and handling

Phone & Fax: 303-258-0670

Email: jpd@peakpeak.com

Or mail this page to Jeffrey Duvall

PO Box 813, Nederland CO 80466

Please send me _____ copies of *Stories of Men, Meaning and Prayer*

Name_____ _____

Address_____

City_____ State_____ Zip_____

____ copies of *Stories of Men, Meaning and Prayer* $_____

$2 per copy for postage and handling $_____

Total amount enclosed $_____

Please do not send cash. Use check or money order. Thank you. Orders will be filled by return mail.

For information about sponsoring a Spirit Camp, workshop or retreat, Jeffrey's youth work, or Men's Leadership Training, write to him at: P.O. Box 813, Nederland, CO 80466, or email him at: jpd@peakpeak.com